The Power to Make Things New

The Power to Make Things New

Edited by Bruce Larson

Messages by

Bruce Larson
F. Dale Bruner
James Forbes
Lloyd Ogilvie
Roberta Hestenes
Cecilio Arrastia
Melicent Huneycutt
Samuel Moffett
Leighton Ford
Thomas Gillespie

WORD BOOKS
PUBLISHER
WACO, TEXAS

A DIVISION OF
WORD, INCORPORATED

THE POWER TO MAKE THINGS NEW

Scripture quotations, unless otherwise identified, are from the King James Version of the Bible. Quotations identified NKJV are from The New King James Version. Copyright © 1979, 1980, 1982, Thomas Nelson, Inc., Publishers. Those identified RSV are from the Revised Standard Version of the Bible, copyrighted 1946, 1952, 1971, 1973 by the Division of Christian Education of the National Council of the Churches of Christ in the U.S.A. Those identified NIV are from the Holy Bible, New International Version. Copyright © 1973, 1978, International Bible Society. Used by permission of Zondervan Bible Publishers. Those identified TEV are from the *Good News Bible*, the Bible in Today's English Version. Copyright © American Bible Society, 1976. Those identified NEB are from the New English Bible. Copyright © The Delegates of the Oxford University Press and the Syndics of the Cambridge University Press 1961, 1970.

Permission to quote from the following sources is gratefully acknowledged.
Lighten Our Darkness by Douglas John Hall. Copyright © 1976 The Westminster Press. Used by permission.
"Listen Lord" by James Weldon Johnson in *Black Poets—A New Anthology*, Edited by Dudley Randall. Copyright © 1971 Bantam Books. Used by permission.

Library of Congress Cataloging in Publication Data

Printed in the United States of America
67898 FG 987654321

Contents

FOREWORD

IMAGINE, IF YOU WILL, THAT YOU ARE A PART OF A GROUP OF concerned people meeting together regularly over a period of years, dreaming and praying about a gathering that could bring together the best resources for renewal in your denomination. The Presbyterian Congress on Renewal came out of just such meetings. The invited speakers were young and old, male and female, pastors and laymen, theologians and clinicians. From the vast and varied resources of our denomination and its leadership, the people whose addresses appear in this book were chosen as being the most representative. As one of them, let me say how honored I am to be in this distinguished company.

Now imagine again, for a moment, that you are one of the persons invited to address this largest Presbyterian gathering ever held in America. How would you react? Aside from feeling humble and afraid of failing, I think you would search your heart, mind, soul, and experience for the deepest convictions you have about who God is, who we are as his covenant people, and what the issues and opportunities are that confront us as a church today. That is the underlying dynamic of each of the messages in this book. No wonder they speak with power and life and reality. Each one is the distillation of a lifetime of costly discipleship. What a string of pearls! Each is valuable in its own way, as it reflects the author's journey of faith. Together they constitute a priceless collection.

But if that were not enough, another dimension makes this book remarkable. It was born out of a *kairos* moment, *kairos* being the Greek word for "time," often translated "moment of opportunity." Unlike *chronos,* the kind of time we measure by clocks and calendars, *kairos* is that "right moment" when God is able to do a mighty work in the life of a believer, or in the life of a church, or in history. This book marks a *kairos* moment in the life of a great denomination.

The Congress in which these addresses were given followed on the reunion of the two great Presbyterian families, separated since the Civil War. The joy of once again becoming one family and the implications for ministry together in Jesus' name are reflected here. But the Congress on Renewal in Dallas in January 1985 also addressed our concern as a denomination over a decade of declining church membership. It is as though with one voice we said, "Enough! Let us be about our Lord's business and extend his kingdom."

It is my conviction that this collection of addresses given on that historic occasion creates a synergy; the whole is greater than the sum of its parts. No single author could have written this book. The wisdom and vision and exhortation we find in these pages could have come only from an eclectic assortment of God's people. I believe the messages in these pages will bless many and that they will help us to hear God's voice and see his footprints in these last days of the twentieth century.

Bruce Larson
University Presbyterian Church
Seattle

1
ALL THINGS NEW
Bruce Larson

Dr. Bruce Larson is the senior pastor of the University Presbyterian Church in Seattle, Washington.

SOME YEARS AGO ELTON TRUEBLOOD ASKED ME, "DO YOU know what the most important word in the Bible is?" Being a spiritual type, I naturally thought of words like "justification," "atonement," and "salvation."

"You're on the wrong track," he said. "The greatest word is *and*. For example, you read, 'Therefore every scribe who has been trained for the kingdom of heaven is like a householder who brings out of his treasure what is new *and* what is old' " (Matt. 13:52 RSV).

"Renewal," Dr. Trueblood told me, "always involves both the new and the old."

When we work and pray for renewal in our church, then,

we need to remember some old things and let God show us some new things. What are some of the old things, the basics?

Significant old things

First of all, we are chosen people. "You did not choose me, but I chose you," Jesus said. He chose you and me just as surely as he chose the disciples while walking the seashore.

Christians today, who worship together, did not choose each other. That gives us problems sometimes. We look around at the folks in our pews: we see Republicans and Democrats, liberals and conservatives, high-church and low-church people. All Christians are peacemakers, but some are peacemakers who believe in securing "peace through strength" and others prefer unilateral disarmament. You have to be careful. You might be sitting next to your ideological opposite.

The early disciples probably had the same difficulty. The twelve followed Jesus, but they had misgivings about each other. They may have asked, "Lord, why did you choose him?" Jesus would have answered, "What is that to you? Follow me."

We Christians have not chosen one another. And that, in itself, is a witness to the world. The world cannot figure out who we are because we do not have all the usual social or political causes in common. We are simply chosen by the one and same and only Lord.

The second old truth, helpful to renewal, is that the gospel is good news. The word *gospel* means good news. A psychiatrist friend told me about getting a postcard from a vacationing patient. The postcard read, "Having a wonderful time! Why?" I'm afraid many of us have been in churches that reflect that attitude. We feel guilty when we feel good.

We could say the gospel is like a two-sided coin—and one of the sides is not good news. John the Baptist proclaimed truth when he said, "Listen, God knows what you're doing and if you don't quit, you're going to hell."

But that's only one side. Jesus turned the coin over. The good news is that God loves us and is on our side. He doesn't want us to go to hell. God wants us to dwell with him now and forever. If we want to go to hell we'll have to fight our way there. In his classic, *The Great Divorce*, C. S. Lewis claimed no one is sent to hell. People go there by choice. At the end of life or beyond, God doesn't contend with us any more. He finally says, "Have it your way."

So evangelism ought to be easy and fun. It is good news. You can tell the worst person you know, "Friend, God loves you." That doesn't mean God likes what that person is doing or who he is at that moment, but John 3:16 is our Magna Carta: "God so loved the world, that he gave his only begotten Son. . . ." The ancient rabbis understood this long before the gospel was made flesh. They believed that a legion of angels goes before every human being proclaiming, "Behold, the image of God!" Tell that to the person you like the least at work on Monday morning.

A third old truth concerns the personal God. God is not a concept or a left-brain truth. Left-brain truth is logical and orderly, arrived at by adding up columns and relying on graphs and charts. Right-brain truth is intuitive, poetic, mysterious, and creative. Both are valid, but you don't relate to someone with your left brain. You can't figure out on a chart, for instance, whether or not you should marry that person standing in the wings. You've got to use your right brain. A marriage commitment to another person is not simply a matter of logic.

Now, whatever else God is, he is a person. And the Bible

is not a book of theological formulae and equations. The Bible is a chronicle written by faithful people, under the power of the Holy Spirit, telling about encounters of a God with individuals, families, nations, and the world. It's God, the Person, in dialogue with his people.

God spoke to Moses from the burning bush and said, "Moses, I want you to go down to Egypt and lead my people out." Moses could have said, "I understand that concept. I believe in the theology of liberation." But God didn't ask Moses to believe in the theology of liberation. Moses was personally to go and lead the Israelites out of Egypt.

Moses understood it was not an intellectual exercise. God was asking him to risk his life and Moses had excuses. "I'm wanted for murder in Egypt," he said. "And I've got a family here. I've got children and sheep and my father-in-law needs me. Besides, I flunked homiletics and I stutter."

Think again of marriage. Suppose someone said to you, "I love you. Will you marry me?" It would be inappropriate to answer, "True." That is what a Catholic priest would say about marriage. He believes in the concept of marriage. In accepting a marriage proposal, we are not merely giving assent to a concept, we are committing ourselves to someone else. And that is exactly what God is asking us, to give him our lives. The appropriate answer is yes or no, not true or false.

I'm convinced our church is full of people who have loved the Lord all their lives, served him, and said, "True, true"—and have never met him. Tip O'Neill, the senator, tells a wonderful story about a chance encounter he had while passing through the Denver airport a while back. A man came up and began to engage him in conversation. They had talked for about five minutes when the man said,

"Say, I don't think you remember me, do you?" "No, I really don't," said the senator. "You see, I'm so well known. I have this big shock of white hair and this large red nose, and I'm on the TV news two or three times a week. A lot of people recognize me, but I can't keep track of all the folks I meet. Who are you?"

"We met at a dinner party about six weeks ago in Washington," was the reply. "My name is Robert Redford."

The good news is that God is not like Tip O'Neill. When you say yes to the Lord, he is *not* going to say, "You know, I know so many people, I have forgotten who you are." He's been waiting for you for a long time and he says, "Come home." For Christians, truth is a person and faith is a verb. Faith is what you do in response to the ultimate Person.

There is a fourth truth we need to rediscover: that the kingdom of God is here and now. The Holy Spirit is the present tense of God. Our hope is not in some future condition. Eternal life begins here and now and it never ends.

Jesus told a parable about the wise and foolish virgins. The foolish virgins had no oil in their lamps when the bridegroom arrived. The only way to understand the parable is to realize that oil, in the Old Testament, represented joy. So some of the virgins had oil—joy—when the kingdom came, and some did not. Those that didn't have oil said, "Wait a minute. We'll run out to the Seven-Eleven and get some. Be right back." But it was too late.

We shouldn't wait either. As a friend of mine says, "If you don't like now, you're going to hate heaven." Heaven begins now.

A fifth and final old truth is the priesthood of all believers. There are not two classes. There is no ultimate clergy and lay distinction. There is no missionary and missionary-supporter distinction.

Paul and Barnabas weren't professional missionaries. They were two friends in the church at Antioch, a church that prayed and fasted about whom to send out to share the good news. The Spirit seemed to say, "Paul and Barnabas," and Paul and Barnabas went.

Today as then, missionaries are not a separate class. The church I pastor has sent out some of the most unlikely people, some who would never get by a mission recruitment board, and they have been remarkably effective. They simply go with love, caring, and openness. They go for a few years or a few months and they discover that God can use them. Our church looks forward to a time when one requirement for membership will be a willingness to consider a short- or long-term mission.

Evangelists are not a separate class either. We recently abolished the evangelism committee of our church. It's amazing how many new members are added in spite of that. But did you ever read in the book of Acts about an evangelism committee—a group set up to call on all of those who dropped by on the day of Pentecost? Every believer is an evangelist.

As all believers are missionaries and evangelists, all believers are ministers. Ministry takes place between believers, and the world is watching to see how we treat each other. They are leery of us because they see our indifference and lack of intimacy. When believers genuinely care for each other, the world will beat down our doors to belong.

Our call to priesthood includes a call to be prophets. A prophet is simply a change agent for the Holy Spirit, someone who says, "God has a better way of doing business in this factory or school or government office."

Significant new things

These are all old, and important, truths. God wants us to discover new things as well. In 2 Corinthians 5:17 we read these words: "Therefore, if any one is in Christ, he is a new creation; the old has passed away, behold, the new has come" (RSV). And from Revelation 21:5: " 'Behold, I make all things new' " (RSV). All things new!

Most of the major institutions in our western world are now imploding. I was intrigued by *Time* magazine's choice for Man of the Year, Peter Ueberroth. Why was he Man of the Year? Because he managed the unmanageable and turned the Olympic Games in Los Angeles into a success. The issue of *Time* recognizing Ueberroth also featured several men and women who are young change agents. *Time* is pointing up the need for people who can help to revitalize our society. Our world is crying out for people who will discover new and better ways.

Jesus Christ wants to give his church a vision of a new society. The world is desperately in need of Christ's creativity and his compassion, as expressed through his people. His people are the salt and light and leaven of the earth. Think of just a few of the many important areas of modern life to which Christians can bring a new vision.

We need a new vision for medicine. Medical scientists have made many brilliant advances in treating the final stages of illness. Granger Westberg, a Lutheran pastor and one of the pioneers in wholistic health, speaks whimsically of three stages of illness: "First, you're a little bit sick, then you're more sick, and then you're real sick." The problem is that doctors rarely see the patient until he or she is "real sick."

Most illness begins when we're a "little sick," and has

causes other than the biophysical—broken relationships, negative attitudes, and destructive lifestyles. The illness progresses until it ends up in an organ. Doctors find themselves doing end-organ medicine at which they are very skilled. A new approach to medicine would begin to deal with illness at a much earlier stage, before it's even what we now consider a medical problem.

Loneliness is called the number one killer in America by James Lynch of Johns Hopkins University. Viktor Frankl is convinced that purpose is the determining factor in health, and that without purpose we may die prematurely. Karl Menninger believes that love is the medicine for the sickness of the world, that we get sick because we cannot give or receive love. Norman Cousins, teaching at UCLA Medical School, says the absence of joy causes illness. Jerrold Michael, dean of the school of public health at the University of Hawaii, believes that the major cause of most illness is a chosen, destructive lifestyle.

The medical profession is talking about loneliness, lifestyle, the lack of purpose, love, or joy, and not one of these problems is biophysical. They are all spiritual, which means the church could become the right arm of medicine, helping people deal with the early stages of illness.

We need a new vision for law. Today, America is the most litigious society in all of history. In Scandinavia, there are three hundred lawsuits a year for every one hundred thousand people. In America there are five thousand. In the United States we have one lawyer for every four hundred people. Great Britain has one for every fourteen hundred, Germany one for every two thousand, and Japan one for every ten thousand. Yet America is supposed to be the most Christian nation in the world.

Warren Burger, Chief Justice of the Supreme Court,

told a group of attorneys, "Tell your clients that going to court is the last resort. Avoid it at all costs." Litigation is terribly expensive, and not only in terms of money. The anger and the unwillingness to forgive disrupts community and upsets individuals physically and emotionally as well as spiritually.

In Seattle, some Christian attorneys started the Christian Conciliation Society. They train teams of laypeople to hear cases for those Christians who want to avoid the cost and delay of courts. In the early stages of this ministry, they discovered something. Most Christians, caught in a legal dispute, never even thought of forgiving each other. It's not that the idea has been rejected. It has never even been considered.

Rather than "forgive our debtors," we sue. Where will the new alternatives to the legal system come from if not from the church of Jesus Christ, where forgiveness is to be the very basis of lifestyle?

We need a new vision for psychiatry and counseling. By the power of the Holy Spirit, lay witness, and the supportive community, Alcoholics Anonymous has done what pastors, psychiatrists, and doctors could not do: controlled alcoholism for countless people. Paul Tournier, Swiss physician and writer, believes that the majority of those now seeking professional counseling could be helped by the same thing Alcoholics Anonymous provides. People who suffer need someone who has traveled that road and can say, "Yes, the pain is excruciating. Let me suggest some things you can do and things you ought not to do. Believe and pray, and you're going to make it. I did." The power of the laity to help fellow-sufferers is enormous.

We need a new vision for education. In the nation's history, we've never spent more on education and received less.

More money or bigger schools is not the solution. We need something else. Arthur Combs, head of the department of education at the University of Florida, told a group of educators, "You and I know that we cannot make good teachers in our educational classes. Good teachers have two qualities. They love themselves and they love their students; and with those two qualities learning will be inevitable in the classroom." What is the source of attributes like that? The gospel—the good news that we're loved and the mandate to love other people. Education is basically a spiritual experience and the new wave of teaching will reflect that fact. It will be more costly, not in money—but in lives expended. Where will the new breed of educators come from if not from the church?

We need a new vision for business. The business community now understands that all successful buying and selling is people-related. I hate shopping in general, but there's one store I enjoy. It's one of the most successful on the West Coast. The personnel department hires clerks who care about customers more than merchandise. The age, sex, or background does not matter. If you're a people-lover, you can learn to sell.

It makes sense. Life is relational. A successful airline is based in Seattle. The president is a Christian, and I asked him, "What are you doing right?" He didn't seem to know. One of the airline's flight attendants is a member of our church, and I asked her that same question.

"I'll tell you why we're making money," she said. "The president knows the names of all the baggage handlers, the ticket sellers, the flight personnel. He walks around and visits us. We feel so cared for that we care for the passengers, and that makes for repeat business." Business is beginning to understand that people are lonely; they want to be cared for and loved. Once again, it is the church that can provide the motivational force for that love and concern.

On the edge

What, then, is the church—old and new? It is the people called, chosen, under orders, to bring the good news of a personal God who loves us, who offers us life now that will never end, and full partnership in the transformation of the world.

I see a church in this land where God's compassionate, caring people will stream out of his sanctuaries Sunday after Sunday to be leaven in society, infiltrating every corridor of public life with better ideas. And the God of Abraham and the God of Isaac and the God of Jacob will have a new name in our time. He will be the God of Bill and Mary, the God of John and Helen, of you and me and our neighbors. He'll be known as the God who cares and creates all things new through his people.

This is the beginning of a new and mighty day, when the wind and fire of the Holy Spirit will sweep the land. We are on the edge of a great adventure.

2
A PARABLE RETOLD
F. Dale Bruner

Dr. F. Dale Bruner is the George and Lyda Wasson
Professor of Religion at Whitworth College, Spokane,
Washington.

THE PARABLE OF THE PRODIGAL SON HAS BEEN CALLED THE gospel within the gospel, the most beautiful short story ever told. It is found only in Luke's Gospel (15:11–32). At the heart of this story Jesus has described in words—as he described in the deeds of his life, death, and resurrection—what the heart of God the Father is like. The parable speaks of a human father, but Jesus is telling it from close acquaintance with God the Father. It is worthwhile to consider the story, line by line.

A tale of two sons

Now a certain man had two sons (v. 11).

This parable has come home to me recently. I have two sons. One is out of adolescence, and one should be. It is remarkable to me how close to type my two boys are. Like so many oldest children, my older son is the "good one." (The good one turns out to be bad in this story, so "good" belongs in quotation marks.) Our second son is more spunky and rebellious. Parents think of obedient, mature-acting older children as somehow better, but it is striking that the "good" older brother is the deep problem in this story. Under consideration now, though, is the younger.

Inheritances

The younger of the two sons came to his father, and he said to him, "Father, please give me that part of the inheritance which is mine" (v. 12).*

The younger brother came to his father and said, "Father." I'm pleased that he addresses him that way. The older brother's speech at the end of the parable is not as respectful.

But the younger brother asks, "Father, please give me that part of the inheritance which belongs to me." Isn't this the vocabulary of many sons to their fathers: "Give me"? Sometimes we fathers have the feeling that we're loved more for what we have than for what we are. It was not entirely thoughtful for the younger brother to ask for his inheritance ahead of time. Our older son recently needed money for graduate school. At one point of desperation he came to us and said, "Would it be all

---

* The Scriptures in italics in this chapter are the author's own translation from the Greek.

right to ask grandpa for a part of my inheritance ahead of time?" We said, "Fred, that wouldn't be good to your grandfather. It's a little like asking him to drop dead."

The loving moves

And the father gave to both boys the family inheritance (v. 12).

Three times in this story the father makes loving moves: the first comes here. It happens at a surprising time, after the insensitive expression of the son. But we must notice it, because it is part of the father's nature. The father agrees to the son's request. He gave them—both boys—the family inheritance.

The first loving thing the father did was let his younger boy go. He saw the rebellious gleam in his son's eye. He knew that his boy's intentions were not good. He could have given him a moral lecture or denied him an early inheritance. But apparently there comes a time in a parent's life when one lets go. In the first chapter of Romans, Paul calls this "letting go" by God—"God gave them up." But Luke seems to be describing this letting go as a part of the love of God.

The Greek here translated "the family inheritance" could also be translated "the family living." The word in question is *bios,* denoting life at its most basic. (The English word *biology* is drawn from it.) The story, then, presents a fine doctrine of creation. God creates us and then gives us free rein. If we want to go, if we don't want to stick around the house, he lets us go.

The waste

Not many days thereafter the son took absolutely everything he had, turned it into cash, and took off for a far country. And there he wasted his substance in reckless living (v. 13).

This boy wanted to get as far away as possible, as soon as possible. (Incidentally, was the elder brother part of the reason for the younger brother wanting to leave? We learn a lot about the unpleasant elder brother in his brief speech at the end of the story and we ought to take it into account.) "Not many days thereafter"—meaning as soon as possible—"he took everything and converted it into cash," which may have meant selling the third of the farm his father gave him.

He "took off for a far country." It is interesting that Jesus never uses the words *sin* or *grace*, or any of the other traditional and marvelous theological terms in this parable. The story is human, with earthy words. "Far country" is a classic picture of rebellion.

The son went into the far country and "wasted his substance in reckless living." Economists define sin as waste, and we say idiomatically, "he got wasted." We all know of men and women who have great minds and waste them, or bodies that are specimens of health and waste them. Opportunities are wasted. "Waste" is an excellent description of the lost life. This boy wasted his substance, his inheritance, his being—his *bios*—on reckless living.

Going under

Now when he had spent everything, a famine hit that country and the boy began to go under. And he went out and he joined himself to one of the citizens of that country, who in turn sent him out to feed his pigs. And the boy was longing to fill his belly with the pods the pigs were eating. And no one gave him a blessed thing (vv. 14–16).

When it rains it pours. He has spent everything, and now the environment gives out. I have to be careful in stating this, but if it had gone well in the far country and if God's providence had not allowed a famine, maybe the son would not have returned home. Can we sometimes interpret our own catastrophes as the love of God, not his wrath? Do catastrophes sometimes bring us home?

When the son began to go under, "he went out and joined himself to one of the citizens of that country." I admire this boy in that he at least looked for work. He didn't wire home for money. He had a little initiative; he got a job feeding pigs. This, of course, is a mark of degradation for the Orthodox Jew.

And it got so bad that he began to long to fill his belly with the pods the pigs were eating. A lot of our longings in our own "far countries" are about this high and about this noble. Our hearts go out to persons lost in "far countries," for that for which they long is not really substantial. It is way beneath their human dignity.

The last thing to give out on the boy was other people. First his own substance gave out, and then his environment. His last illusion might have been that people are basically good. When he had money, he had plenty of friends. But when he was not doing so well it was hard to find those friends. "The poor man is hated even by his own neighbor, but the rich has many friends" (Prov. 14:20 NKJV). "Nobody gave him a thing." The human race is not God, and the human race does not come through in the clutch.

The turnabout

Now, when the boy came to himself he said, "How many hired hands of my father are swimming in bread and I'm here starving. I'm dying. I know what I'll do. I'll get up and I'll go back to my father and I'll say, 'Father, I sinned against heaven and against you. I don't deserve to be called your son anymore. Make me like one of your hired hands'" (vv. 17–19).

At this point comes the line that begins to depict the turnabout: "when the boy came to himself." On the whole, the self does not get a good press in the New Testament. We are told, for example, to deny our selves; the person who seeks his self will lose it, the person who loses his self will find it. But this is one of those few texts indicating that, when we consult our self, we are only one step from God.

Tertullian said that the *anima naturaliter Christianus*—the human soul is naturally Christian. That is a dangerous sentence. We don't believe, like Unitarians, that there is a divine spark within, and that all one needs is to gently fan the spark. But there is a sense in which the self is God's creature, and when we consult our best personal interests we begin to think of the Father.

"When the boy came to himself he said, 'How many hired hands of my father are swimming in bread.'" Pelagius and Augustine debated this text. Pelagius said it is the human person—not God—who must take the initiative, and until the son came back the father didn't do anything. Since the father here represents God, the human will comes first in conversion.

But notice what the son is thinking of: "How many hired hands of my father. . . ." The memory of a good father beckons him home. If that father had not been just to his employees, if that father had not given decent food to those who worked for him, the son would never have gone back. The father had implanted the good memory of his own character in his son's conscience, and it is the father, through that memory, who beckons the son.

Augustine wins. God's grace comes first and then our response. Without that grace we do not have the will, we do not have the power, we do not have even the desire to go back to the Father.

The boy says he is starving. He is dying. When a person can say, "I'm dying," he is not far from the Father. "I'm dying. I am not at all where I am supposed to be: I am a son, I am a daughter of God, the Father, and yet I am dying. I know what I will do. I will get up, I will go back to my Father. . "

I admire the son for being absolutely straight. He invents no excuses. He is not blaming the weather or the famine, or saying that his friends did not come through. He is going to tell his father he sinned. And somehow that confession has its own power. When we come clean, when we confess our sins, "he is faithful, he is just, he will forgive us our sins and cleanse us from all unrighteousness" (1 John 1:9).

Notice Jesus' realism at this point. The boy is not portrayed as having noble motives for his return. He is not going back because he broke his father's heart. He is going back because he is not eating well and he wants a better meal. Jesus knows human beings. Our motives in coming to Christ are not always as high as they ought to be. But God will take us no matter how we come. He will use every secular, material, or physical motive to return us home. Jesus does not describe the motive of the younger son as any more noble than wanting to have a good meal.

Starting back

So the boy got up and he started back (v. 20).

This text was a deep help to my wife and me after ten years as missionaries in the Philippines. We were emotionally, physically, and spiritually exhausted. The ten years had not been happy or productive. I had not been a good missionary. And I did not want to have ten more years of failure. But I did not have the physical or spiritual energy to fulfill whatever conditions were necessary for God to bless and help make my teaching better. This text helped me. It said, "Just start back. The Father does all the rest." As is clear from the next line.

The terrible sprint

Now when he was still a long way off his father saw him, and his heart went out to him, and he ran and threw his arms around his son, and he kissed him much (v. 20).

This text says to all who are weary and who do not feel close to God: just face the Father; he will do the rest. This is the greatest of the father's three moves of love. "Now while he was still a long way off. . . ." The Greek for "long way off" is the same word used earlier in the text for "far" country. It conveys the idea that the father, every night after work, stood on the brow of the hill and looked out over the valley and hills, searching the distant far country for his son.

And one day he could tell that one particular dot was his son, so while the boy "was still a long way off" the father saw his son "and his heart went out to him, and he ran. . . ." Picture the father running down the valleys and up the hills toward his son. And finally, he threw himself on his boy and "embraced him and kissed him much."

The major theological criticism of this parable is that there is no Cross in it, that it tends to be sentimental. It is said to depict a God who is so much love that there is no justice or holiness left in him. The father's run and unconditional forgiveness are thought to say to all the wayward, in effect, "You can run away and there won't be any price; there won't be any probation. Simply come back and I will wink at everything you have done."

This is fair criticism, but I submit that in the father's run there is an intimation of Jesus' coming to the cross. The father's run is that terrible sprint from heaven to the wood. There is holiness; there is justice. Someone had to pay a price and the Father paid it. "God was in Christ, reconciling the world unto himself" (2 Cor. 5:19).

So the father ran to his son. And his next action is amazing. He did not wait for his son's apology or confession. All he wanted was the son. He was thrilled that his son is there, and he threw his arms around the boy before the boy could get more than a few words out. He embraced his son before the son completed his prepared confession of sin (contrast verses 18, 19, and 21).

The good caress

The boy said, "Father, I have sinned against heaven and you, and I don't deserve to be called your son." The father interrupted him and said to his servants, "Quick, get the best robe and put it on him. Put the ring on his finger, and put sandals on his feet. And go get the fatted calf, kill it, and let's have a party because my son was dead—he's come back to life. He was lost, and he's been found" (vv. 21–24).

The father interrupts his son's confession and tells the servants to get the boy a robe, a ring, and sandals. Interestingly, the father never speaks verbally and directly to the younger son in this entire parable. He speaks, as it were, physically and sacramentally. The sacraments are God's hugs—they are God physically approaching and touching us. The main thing a father gives to his son, and the best way he communicates with his son, is by touching him. This father is saying many things about God the Father by what he does. The "best robe," for example, is a marvelous picture of absolute justification. As the Heidelberg Catechism puts it, God imputes and grants to us the perfect righteousness, satisfaction, and holiness of Jesus Christ, as if we had never ever sinned. But the robe of righteousness is not all.

The ring symbolized power. It was used as a kind of signature: with it the son had power to sign and validate official documents. This is an excellent symbol of the power and the gift of the Holy Spirit, who is given to us in baptism and who is continually reappropriated by simple faith. We have power to act in God's name through the gift of the ring of the Holy Spirit. We are sanctified.

Lastly, the boy is given sandals. This reminds us of the black spiritual, "I've got shoes, you've got shoes, all God's children got shoes. . . ." Slaves were not able to wear shoes and longed for their shodding. Shoes are now given to this boy. He is treated as a son. The returned prodigal is rich beyond deserving. He has the robe of righteousness, the ring of power, and the shoes of adoption.

We, too, are rich, though we sometimes fail to recognize it. We in the Reformed tradition sometimes neglect God's hugs—the sacraments that are God touching and loving us. (Our Confessions do not neglect them.) We need a deeper appreciation of simple baptism, for example, for we receive many gifts in baptism, not the least God's Holy Spirit. How much we should appreciate the open heaven of justification, the Dove Spirit of sanctification, and the voice saying, "My son," which Christ's baptism gives us

(Matt. 3:16, 17). Jesus inaugurated baptism in his own person, and in baptism we were given the three gifts of justification, sanctification, and adoption, of robe, ring, and sandals.

Baptism is one great sacrament. The second one is the Eucharist, or the Lord's Supper. I hope I am not over-interpreting the parable when I find in the father's meal for his son an intimation of our churches' festal communion meal. The *Eu* in Eucharist means "good," and *charis* is the root of our English word *caress*. The Lord's Supper is the "good caress"; in this sacrament God comes to us spiritually and physically and touches us and says, "I love you."

Catholics call our Protestant church services "dry masses." They say we get half way there and then stop. We minister the Word but we don't touch. It will be a good day when we again observe the sacrament every Sunday, as Luther and Calvin intended. Then our words, our reading of Scripture and preaching, which are God's very Word, will be confirmed by our simple deeds, our administering of God's touching sacraments, which are God's very arms. (See the beautiful tributes to the meanings of baptism and the Lord's Supper in the compact ecumenical classic, the "Lima Text," *Baptism, Eucharist, and Ministry,* "Faith and Order Paper No. 3," Geneva: World Council of Churches, 1982.)

The Presbyterian

Now the elder brother was out in the field, and as he came in toward the house he heard the sounds of music and dancing, and he summoned one of the servants and said, "What's going on in there?" The servant said, "Your brother is back, and your

father has killed the fatted calf because he's home in one piece."
The brother was furious. He would not go in, so the father
came out and pled with him (vv. 25–28).

The older brother was out in the field. The Greek word
for "elder" or "older" here is *presbuteros.* The elder son
is literally the "Presbyterian" son. The Presbyterian, naturally, was out in the field, dutifully working. He was doing
what he ought to be doing, and as he approached the
house he heard the sounds of music and dancing. Such
sounds are always suspicious to Puritan types. Remember
H. L. Mencken's definition of a Puritan as a person with
a haunting fear that someone, somewhere, is happy.
So to the elder son's ears the situation did not sound
auspicious.

He summoned his servant and asked what was going
on. The servant told him that his brother was home and
his father had killed the fatted calf to celebrate. The older
brother, infuriated, won't go into the house. And here it
is actually easier to love the prodigal, who at least headed
home. Not so the self-righteous elder brother.

Then comes the third and last loving move of the father
in the parable. "The father came out and pled with him."
This little line means many things, but it means at least
this: God also loves Christians. This is good news. I know
God loves the sinner; the whole Scripture is filled with
that message. But does God also love self-righteous Presbyterians and other Christians? This text says much more
than that but nothing less.* God also loves *Christians* who,

---

* Note. I should have spelled out this "much more." The major criticism of
my exposition (and of the Congress generally) was the absence of a sufficient
note of repentance. This criticism is well taken, and I repent. I should have
said right here that Jesus' depiction of the elder brother also means that good

like this elder brother, stuck in sin and pride, refuse to join the party. That is a love I can hardly understand. "Amazing grace, how sweet the sound, that saved a self-righteous prig like me. . . ."

The speech of grievance

But the boy said, "Look, I have slaved for you all these years. I have never broken one of your commandments. And yet what do I get for it? You've never even killed a shriveled up old goat for me so that I could have a party with my friends. But when this son of yours comes back who has blown the family inheritance on whores, you kill a fatted calf for him" (vv. 28-30).

The father pled with the boy, and then the older boy gave a speech. The boy's opening words are not as respectful as those of the younger brother at the beginning of the story who at least said "Father." The older son speaks as if his father can't see, as if the father is in fact blind or stupid. "Look," he commands, and continues, "I have *slaved* for you all these years. . . ." Slavery is how he conceives of his work with his father. "I have never broken one of your commandments," he says (what about the commandment of love?).

"Yet," the elder brother complains, "you've never even killed a shriveled up old goat for me so that I could have a party with my friends. But when this son of yours. . . ." Notice that it's not "this brother of mine." The same thing

---

older brothers, like good Presbyterians and other Christians, are sometimes the greatest sinners of all—in our pride, in our social and moral blindness, and in our failure to have a heart for all our other brothers and sisters, lost or coming home.

happens in our home. I say, "Kathy, do you know what your son did?" There is a shift in language, as if my son's misdeeds are my wife's responsibility or fault.

The angry son finishes, "When this son of yours comes back who has blown the family inheritance on whores, you kill a fatted calf for him." The eldest is saying, in effect, "I don't get you. I think you are weak." Many husbands say this to their wives. I do.

In a sense, the father in this story depicts a mother's love more than a typical father's love. I don't intend to be sexist, but I think that a mother's love is more often unconditional than the love of most fathers I know. It has been said that most mothers understand home as a nest and most fathers understand it as a boot camp. The father's question is usually, "Did you get a job? Do you have summer work?" The mother asks, "Are you happy? Are you loved?" So there is something unusual about the love of the father in this parable. But the oldest boy thinks his father lacks character and backbone. He thinks he lacks justice and that he is hurting the community by his example.

Come into the house

The father said to his son, "My child, you are constantly with me. Absolutely everything I have is yours. But it was right for us to have this party because this your brother was dead and now he is alive. He was lost but he's been found" (vv. 31–32).

The father replied gently, *"My child,* you are constantly with me." Notice the present tense verbs: "You *are* constantly with me. . . . everything I *have* is yours." (Not: "You *were* before your cruel speech.") The angry speech the son has just given has made no difference in the father's benevolence. "You are constantly with me. Absolutely everything I have is yours. But it was right for us to have this party because this your brother was dead and now he is alive. He was lost but he's been found."

This, finally, is the message of the story. To all prodigals and younger siblings, chronologically or spiritually: Turn from your pigsties and come home; the Father is good. And to all elder brothers and sisters, chronologically or spiritually: Turn from your self-righteousness, and come into the house. Enjoy your brothers and sisters; the Father is good.

3
RESTORATION AND CELEBRATION
James Forbes

Dr. James Forbes is the Joe R. Engle Professor of Preaching at Union Theological Seminary, New York, New York.

Now his elder son was in the field; and as he came and drew near to the house, he heard music and dancing. And he called one of the servants and asked what this meant. And he said to him, "Your brother has come, and your father has killed the fatted calf, because he has received him safe and sound." But he was angry and refused to go in. His father came out and entreated him, but he answered his father, "Lo, these many years I have served you, and I never disobeyed your command; yet you never gave me a kid, that I might make merry with my friends. But when this son of yours came, who has devoured your living with harlots, you killed for him the fatted calf!" And he said to him, "Son, you are always with me, and all

*that is mine is yours. It was fitting to make merry and be glad,
for this your brother was dead, and is alive; he was lost, and
is found."*   Luke 15:25–32 RSV

What do you think of the elder brother in the parable of
the prodigal son? Not everyone has the same reaction to
the elder brother. I learned that the hard way once when
I preached a sermon on Luke 15. In the sermon I had
acknowledged quite candidly that I didn't like the older
brother one bit. I said he was judgmental and jealous,
moralistic and legalistic. I said he was an insensitive, suspicious, narrow-minded, haughty, holier-than-thou, Calvinis-
tic workaholic. . . .

One woman was kind enough to wait until after I had
shaken hands and received greetings at the door. Then
she pulled me aside privately and told me that she was
sick and tired of preachers dumping on the elder brother.
She said, "Somebody has to stay home and work to support
those who are all too ready to waste the hard-earned resources of other people. And why should an immoral
scoundrel come out smelling like a rose, while the decent,
dutiful son gets nothing but condemnation? It was all I
could do to keep from walking out on you," she said, "and
if any other preacher does it, I promise I will walk out."

So now I check with the congregation before getting
into a sermon about the elder brother. I inquire seriously,
"How do you feel about the elder brother?" I think I have
grown out of some of my judgmental, insensitive, and
holier-than-thou attitude concerning him. I am now able
to appreciate his diligence and his faithfulness in duty. It
is good that there is somebody who will work. We have
too many people who are willing to let other people do
the job. It is commendable that while others are exploring

exotic corners of the earth, there's somebody who day after day fulfills primary responsibility to the home place.

But, although I appreciate him more, there *is* one thing about the elder brother that has lured preachers and lay-people to dump on him. All his hard work notwithstanding, he had not come to understand what really mattered to his father. Or if he understood intellectually, he had not absorbed the spirit of his father. Perhaps something deep inside him, something quite strong, was at war against the will of his father.

"But he was angry and refused to go in," the text reads. He resisted the entreaty of his father. The pleading of the father, so far as we can tell by the time the story ends, fell on a hardened heart and closed mind. Just think of it. What a pity that all of the time, energy, and effort of the older brother now cast a negative light, because he didn't know what really mattered to his father.

It may be valuable for us to look at what that father was like, at what did matter to that father. The sense of the parable, after all, is that the father here represents God. It might not have been easy for the elder brother to get in step even if he had known what the father's great concern was. It may not be easy for us to get in step after we know the concern and passion of the Father. But it is important that we not find ourselves in the place of the elder brother. It's important that we not spend all our time and energy for God, and then find out we never understood what he wanted. We need to know: What is on the heart of God for us?

The heart of God

There are clues to the heart of God outside the parable, in the first verses of the chapter. "Now the tax collectors and sinners were all drawing near to him. And the Pharisees and the scribes murmured, saying, 'This man receives sinners and eats with them' " (vv.1,2 RSV). The Pharisees and scribes did not understand Jesus. And, seeing this, Jesus told the story of the lost sheep, the story of the lost coin, and the story of the lost boy—the prodigal.

The common element in all three of these stories is that something that belongs in a certain place has been separated from the context in which it belongs. The sheep has been separated from the flock; the coin is gone from its purse; and the son has left his home. I have the impression that Jesus, to get his point across, had to tell story after story after story.

These three stories are prompted by the Pharisees, who murmur because Jesus reaches out to those who are separated from legal and ritual purity. Ironically, the word *Pharisee* itself meant "separated one." The Pharisees may have been separated more profoundly than they knew, for apparently they did not understand the Spirit of God.

The Pharisees, then, are separated. The tax collectors and sinners are separated. The lost sheep, lost coin, and lost boy (or lost boys, if we include the elder brother) are separated. It appears to be the concern of the text that God Almighty, whatever else we may say, has an extraordinary sensitivity about that which belongs and has become separated.

God's obsession

This is the extraordinary fixation of God. God Almighty made this great big beautiful world and called it good. Then he experienced the Fall, the separation and alienation of his creation from himself. Since then, God has had a kind of obsession. He seems to be unusually nervous and anxious and eager about separations. If you believe the prophets, you might also say God is depressed about separations.

There is separation in families where people thought they had it going; they loved each other, pledged their troth one to another at the altar, and then: brokenness. God is sensitive about that.

There is separation in ecclesiastical bodies, separation that strikes to the heart of self-interest and identity. God is sensitive about that.

God is sensitive about black separated from white; black separated from black; Hispanic separated from native American; and First world separated from Second and Third world. Wherever there is brokenness and separation in a context where there was to be wholeness, God is intensely concerned and has a perpetual heartache.

Luke 15 is about a God who—in the face of separation, wherever it is found—goes to work. That is why Jesus was with the tax collectors and the sinners at the start. The scribes and the Pharisees murmured because Jesus received the sinners and ate with them. I once thought Jesus got angry at the Pharisees. But I was wrong about the elder brother, and I was wrong about Jesus' anger. I thought he told his stories to put down the Pharisees. But he told the stories on behalf of the aching, beating heart of God reaching out even to the Pharisees and the scribes. Jesus thought, *If I can tell them a story, or maybe two or three stories, perhaps they'll see how separated they really are, and will see God's acceptance and longing for them.*

So he told his stories. Where a sheep is lost, God reaches out like a shepherd. He searches until he finds and there is restoration. The story of the lost coin has a double meaning, hinting at a broader restoration than some of us yet are prepared to receive. For Jesus, in this story, sneaked in a woman to describe the actions of God. Clearly, God wants to end separation wherever it is: between races, between nations—even between sexes.

And between churches too. The Presbyterian Church (USA) is a restored church. It has ended a separation. What can God have in store for it? Might he have a way of bringing together the conservatives and the liberals in this church? It can't be easy. The Presbyterian Church has fallen. It lost some ground while it was separated, and it is only the miracle of God that it was not more serious than it was. But now that the church is together there is a need for a spiritual restoration.

And if the truth could be known, there is no way the prodigal son could have gotten up if he had never acknowledged that he was down. Do you know in what way the church had gotten down? Are you sensitive to the way in which our own selfish notion of what ought to be has somehow become more important than what God's concern might be?

That brings me back to the elder brother. Truthfully, let's don't be so hard on him. We may have the same problem he did. If the church deals with racism, sexism, classism, ageism—if the church is going to deal with various sins of brokenness and alienation, conservative sins as well as liberal—it is not going to be very cost efficient. And this was exactly, I think, what plagued the elder brother. The tension was there before the prodigal son returned. Remember that the father took good care of and lavished resources on his servants (Luke 15:17). The elder brother may have said to his father, "There isn't anyone who takes such good care of their servants. What is your problem? We're never going to make up for what we lost when my little brother took away his portion of the farm. In this market, it doesn't make sense to do so much for the servants." The elder brother was a good American pragmatist.

But the father was sensitive to conditions of separation and alienation. And so is God. God is inordinately committed to bringing about restoration. He said, "I will do it if it kills me," and it did.

There is nothing in the world that anybody can do that makes God happier than to be sensitive to where restoration is occurring, and then to participate. Where we participate, we can begin to celebrate. As the father in the parable said to the servant, "Bring me the best robe, put a ring on his hand and shoes on his feet. Don't bring McDonald's hamburgers for this: we've got to kill the fatted calf. Let us eat and be merry, for my son that was lost is found; he was dead and he is alive."

"He was dead and he is alive." Dead—alive! Dead—alive! Dead—alive! How Christocentrically those words ring in my ear! Christ died and was resurrected, and he is alive in our midst. He is alive at the table, alive in the pulpit, alive in the choir stand, alive with lay ministries, all over this world! And so we are called to celebrate.

There are problems, of course. This denomination has been separated and bears deep wounds. There is a lot of alienation, a lot of brokenness. Some folks don't even believe that God should love the other folks and, to tell the truth, they don't even see how God loves their own selves.

But still, God says, "Celebrate. Get ready. Do what you can, become my servants." God has arranged a committee, the Committee for the Celebration of Restoration of the Nation. We are recruiting more members for the committee. The qualifications are that you must believe that God cares about separation and must commit yourself to being God's agent of restoration wherever you have influence. You must commit yourself to restoration wherever you have influence and resources, wherever you are— to encourage, to inspire, to heal. In working as an agent of restoration, you, too, will be healed, will be freed of your servitude in the pigpen or the field.

You may wonder, "Can I qualify for the committee? Do I have resources? Do I want to be on it?" The answer is that God will make his resources available to you: spiritual resources. When the Holy Spirit falls upon this united church, nobody will have to come outside and invite you to the committee. You will come in willingly; more than that, eagerly. You will be breaking the door down to get into the celebration of God.

I'm talking about a good time. I'm talking about a glorious church and a beautiful new struggle that has direction and purpose. What a time it is going to be!

So I make a motion, and await your second, a motion that this church will offer itself to be one of God's primary agencies on the Committee for the Celebration of Restoration of the Nation. If you second that motion we don't need a moderator to carry it because it is already being moderated by the Father and the Son and the Holy Spirit, and by all sisters and brothers.

To God be all the glory and all the praise.

4
PERFECT MAKES PRACTICE
Lloyd John Ogilvie

Dr. Lloyd John Ogilvie is the senior pastor of the First Presbyterian Church in Hollywood, California. His message to the Presbyterian Congress on Renewal is presented without editorial revision.

"Therefore you shall be perfect, just as your Father in heaven is perfect."   (Matt. 5:48 NKJV)

"Do you want to be made well?"   (John 5:6 NKJV)

A couple of weeks ago, in preparation for this evening's message, I spent a day calling people registered for this Congress on Renewal. It was a random sampling of the list. I knew some of the people I called but others were complete strangers.

"What's your greatest hope for the Congress on Renewal?" I asked. "What is your vision for our time together for yourself, your local church, and our merged and emerging denomination? What do you expect?"

I was amazed by the wide spectrum of responses. And I suspect they represent the variety of ways you would answer. What do *you* expect?

One pastor I called certainly represents a large portion here tonight. "I'm burned out," he confessed. "I'm coming to Dallas with a little flickering ember in the ashes of my personal and professional life. I really hope that ember will be fanned and fueled into a blaze again."

A woman who pastors a challenging church said she hoped that she would be able to recover the excitement and enthusiasm she had experienced when she was called into the ministry. "Somehow getting through seminary and now trying to bring renewal to a traditional Presbyterian church sure has kicked the joy out of me. What do you do when you lose the joy? What do I want? I need the encouragement of knowing I'm not alone in this battle!"

A middle-aged man put his need differently. "I'm a pastor of a small church. I really need help to revitalize my parish. I'm coming looking for ideas, programs, some direction. So often, I feel the lack of strong direction in our denomination. We need someone to raise the flag. I'd like to be part of a movement!"

A young man just out of seminary was very honest about why he was coming. "I've saved my money for a year to come to Dallas. Why? I guess it's because I'm lonely. I hope to get a boost out of being with some people who aren't ashamed of being committed to Christ and want to pray for and encourage each other."

A woman elder in a church in the East said, "Well, I'm an evangelical, you know. And I won't be satisfied unless the Bible is preached, Jesus is raised up, souls are saved, and you have an invitation at the end of every meeting. That's what I expect!" And with that she hung up.

The next call I made was to a man who referred to himself as a "charismatic Presbyterian." I didn't have to prime him for what he expected from the Congress. "I pray that it will be the greatest outpouring of power since Pentecost! I think our church needs what I needed when I was baptized with the Holy Spirit. We're out of steam, in need of Holy Spirit power and fire. Why don't we let loose, take the cap of reservation off and get filled with power? I hope we'll dance in the aisles!"

A man committed to missions said, "Listen, Lloyd, I'm being sent to that conference by friends who think I need it. But the other day I took out my calculator and figured out all the money that will be spent on the Congress— expenses, travel, and the like—and I figure it goes into the millions. I'd rather we take all that money and send it to feed the starving people in Africa."

Another man who serves on some of the reorganization committees for our new denomination was very frank. "I think this Congress could be a poorly timed 'glitch' in the process of getting our new, united church organized. Honestly, I'll be happy when it's all over."

A denominational legalist sounded a similar note. "Whatever happens at the Congress will be fruitless unless it makes for better Presbyterians to serve the church and the committees of presbytery back home."

But it was a presbytery executive who expressed a deeper longing than the denominational legalist. "I'm sick and tired of all the conflict between the various groups within our denomination. I hope for a healing of the brokenness in the church. I'm coming to the Congress—hoping, praying—that our beloved church will be healed."

And so the responses went—people in deep spiritual need, people with causes to champion, people who want to hear their song played to their tempo, people who long to find the secret of renewal in their own personal lives and in the church, people who are looking for the identifiable language of their theological persuasion, people who hope this will be the most crucial event in the history of American Presbyterianism, and people who will be happy when it's all over and we can get back into our separate and safe camps.

How would you answer the question? What do you expect from our time together here in Dallas?

So often we come to the end of meetings like this and ask the question of ourselves and others in the past tense and with a disappointed tone. "Well, what did you expect?" Usually we don't expect very much and that's usually what we get. A pertinent poem expresses that and raises our expectation. In response to the Father's heart offered with healing love in the Savior—

Filled with a strange new hope they came,
    The blind, the leper, the sick, the lame,
Frail of body and spent of soul
    As many as touched Him were made whole.
On every tongue was the Healer's name
    Throughout the land they spread His fame.
But doubt held tightly to its wooden crutch
    Saying, "We must not expect too much."
Down through the ages the promise came,
    Healing for sorrow, sin, and shame.
Help for the helpless, hope for the blind,
    Healing of body, soul, and mind.
The Lord we worship is still the same,
    With blessings for all who will to claim.

But how often we miss love's healing touch
By saying, "We must not expect too much!"
(*Author unknown*)

The good news is that we cannot expect too much. Whatever is our boldest dream for this Congress—our personal lives, our congregations, our denomination—it is small in comparison to what the Father expects.

Thou art coming to a King,
Large petitions with thee bring;
For His grace and power are such,
None can ever ask too much.

John Newton

Our challenge is to widen our expectations to the broadest reaches of the Father's expectations. And to help us do that, he enlivens our imaginations with the focused vision of what he wants to do here as a provisional demonstration of what he longs to do in the United Presbyterian Church as a whole.

We are all in the process of becoming what we dare to envision with the gift of imagination. It's true for us as individuals and for the church. Our Father has created our cerebral cortex, our thinking brain, with the magnificent endowment of imagination—the ability to form, hold, and marshall our energies to achieve the images he gives us. Imagination is congealed thought and when it is surrendered to our Father's use, it can be the canvas on which he can paint his picture of what he intends for us. But often the canvas is layered with the hardened, cracking, peeling pictures of our own limited expectation. That's why my prayer for us at this Congress is what James Weldon Johnson prayed for the preacher in *Listen Lord!*

Put his eye to the telescope of eternity,
And let him look upon the paper thin walls of time.

Lord, turpentine his imagination,
Fill him full of the dynamic of Thy power,
Anoint him all over with the oil of Thy salvation,
And set his tongue of fire.

I expect nothing less than that tonight. My greatest concern is that the level we seek may not be radical enough. The word *radical* means "to the roots." And the root of newness is in God our Father. True renewal does not come from ecclesiology or Jesusology or charismology or missiology, but from Patrology. *Pater*, Abba Father. Renewal is a Father movement. Only our Father can lift us out of ourselves and heal our brokenness as individuals and as a church.

By the end of my day of calling people to find out what they expected from the Congress, I felt deeply the pain of division in the church today. The major enclaves we find in most local churches and presbyteries were distressingly evident: the denominationalists, the mission-minded, the spiritually depressed elders and pastors, and the great host of people who yearn to be part of a great awakening in the church.

"Let's get it all together again"

Perhaps that is the reason that the last conversation I had on the phone that day was so meaningful to me. A pastor of one of our churches in the South put his response succinctly and with colloquial color. "Lloyd, I just want us all to get it all together again."

I haven't been able to get that off my mind. The man had expressed my deepest hope for this Congress. I turned his expression over in my mind, thinking about the different emphases with which it could be expressed. I want all the Father has to give. And I want that all together with you, beyond our separateness and power struggles.

Again? That leads us to more than the repetition of a cherished memory of some experience in the past. Greater than the god of our experience is a fresh experience of the glory and grace of God our Father. Authentic renewal happens as we return again to the heart of our Father and claim his adoption of us as his children and are drawn anew into the unity and oneness of being brothers and sisters in his family.

H. H. Farmer said, "God our Father is absolute demand and absolute succor." We are accustomed to hearing more about the succor, his gracious love, than we are about the absolute demand of his holiness, righteousness, and judgment. And that may explain why the church needs a Father movement. Revivals and renewal have taken place in history as a result of the church submitting to the authority and discipline of the Father. Then the preaching and experience of his grace in Jesus Christ and his power in the Holy Spirit are truly good news.

I know that from my own experience. The most moving times of renewal for me have come when God the Father forced me to see myself as I truly was. He didn't just deal with surface problems, but penetrated to the citadel of my soul. All the things which were blocking his total command of my life were exposed and had to be confessed. My emptiness had to be admitted, my lack of power acknowledged. My willfulness lanced at the core. And the Father did it out of unqualified, healing love. He is the Refiner of the gold, the Purifier of the silver, the Potter of the clay, and the Surgeon of the soul. He loves us as we are but never leaves us there. The Father cares too much for that.

One of the most moving times of renewal in my life took place on the Mount of Beatitudes above the Sea of

Galilee. I was spending the summer in the area writing a book on the Sermon on the Mount. Each morning I would rise at dawn and drive to the Mount of Beatitudes. There, on the site where Jesus delivered the Sermon on the Mount, I would read a few verses of His message and then try to picture in my mind's eye the Master delivering the words. What had been blunted with familiarity in my mind came alive with fresh intensity and meaning.

I'll never forget the experience of imagining what it must have been like when the disciples and the crowd first heard the bracing promise, "Therefore you shall be perfect, just as your Father in heaven is perfect" (Matt. 5:48). I pictured the astonishment on the faces of the people and their amazed exchanges with each other. I too was startled, as if really hearing the promise for the first time. The rest of the day was spent thinking and praying about what Jesus meant. I was gripped by the realization that the promise is really the secret of continuous, authentic renewal.

Checking my Greek New Testament I was reminded that the Greek word used to record Jesus' Aramaic for *perfect* is *teleioi,* referring to us, and *teleios,* for God. Both come from *telos,* meaning purpose, end, goal, limit. It also is used in the sense of reaching an end, being finished, complete, or mature. A thing is perfect if it meets the purpose for which it was planned; a person is perfect if he or she realizes, and presses on to reach, the purpose for which he or she was born.

In that light what I think Jesus promised is that we shall accomplish our purpose or goal even as the Father accomplishes His. But what is the Father's purpose? To help us fulfill our purpose. His goal is to enable us to live at full potential, living life as he planned it to be lived. We shall be all that he has meant us to be because it is the Father's "good pleasure" to accomplish it.

So the promise of the Father through Christ is not a challenge to human perfectionism but an assurance that there is unlimited power available for us to be his daughters and sons expressing our family likeness by emulating his giving, forgiving, unstintingly generous heart. Irenaeus was on target: "The glory of God is a person fully alive." Or in keeping with the theme of today's emphasis in the Congress on the glory and majesty of God the Father— the triumph of the purpose of God is to reproduce that glory and majesty in us. Awesome? Yes!

The adopting Father

In that light we can understand and appreciate more fully the Father's purpose in the life, message, death, resurrection and present indwelling power of Christ. The total impact of the Incarnation is to bring us into oneness with the Father. He came to us in the Son to show us what it means to be his sons and daughters. Jesus taught us to pray to God as our Father, he revealed what absolute obedience to the Father means, and showed us the "Abba Father" intimacy we were created, chosen, and called to experience. The term "Father" for God is seldom used in the Old Testament. We learned its full meaning from Christ who taught us to say "Your will, not mine, be done," as the secret of growing in fellowship with the Father.

Christ went to the cross with the word *Father* in his heart and on his lips. And there he completed the one, never-to-be-repeated substitutionary sacrifice for our sins.

Sin could well be defined as our rebellion against our Father, our refusal to be his obedient sons and daughters. Sin is anything which stands in the way of the intimate oneness we were created to enjoy with him, and all that misses the mark of his will for us. Through the cross we are exonerated, declared "not guilty." And for what *telos,* purpose? So that we can be fully daughters and sons living abundantly now, and eternally, forever.

But the Father movement in the Incarnation did not end with the crucifixion and resurrection. The triumph over sin and death was only an end of the beginning. Luke captures that dynamic in his opening line of Acts. He refers to the incarnate life of Jesus as what he *"began* to do and teach" (italics mine). Acts is the biblical record of what the risen, reigning Christ continued to do. And spread across its pages is the exciting account of a new breed of humanity who, through what Christ had done in the cross and resurrection and continued to do in them as indwelling Lord, became faithful, obedient daughters and sons of the Father.

Paul catches the wonder of this new creation: "But when the fullness of the time had come, God sent forth His Son, born of a woman, born under the law, to redeem those who were under the law, that we might receive the adoption as sons. And because you are sons, God has sent forth the Spirit of His Son into your hearts, crying out, 'Abba, Father!' Therefore you are no longer a slave but a son, and if a son, then an heir of God through Christ" (Gal. 4:4–7 NKJV). The ministry of the Spirit in us is to help us claim our status and live with freedom and joy. Again, in Romans 8:15–17, Paul sounds the triumphant note: "For you did not receive the spirit of bondage again to fear, but you received the Spirit of adoption by whom we cry out, 'Abba, Father.' The Spirit Himself bears witness with our spirit that we are children of God, and if children, then heirs—heirs of God and joint heirs with Christ . . ." (NKJV).

All this is offered us as a gift to help us accomplish our purpose of being his sons and daughters. That's the

Father's ultimate purpose. Renewal is a recall to that purpose, an incisive encounter with him and his relentless efforts to make us like him.

The neglected Father

And yet, for many of us, God our Father is neglected. We can take a gentle Jesus or the inspiration of the Spirit, but resist the absolute demands of the Father. Helmut Thielicke talked about the *waiting* Father and Thomas Smail of the *forgotten* Father. My concern is for the *neglected* Father. In many of our churches the lack of straightforward teaching and preaching about the demands of a holy Father makes life a trial without a judge. The result is self-justification or self-condemnation. In either case we become our own judges. And when that happens the preaching of grace loses its power. We come to church to have our needs met. But most of those needs are to prop up the perpendicular pronoun. We want strength and courage to accomplish our plans and purposes. We've changed Jesus' invitation to read, "Come to Me and I will give you what you want!"

And by inference, (and unlike this morning's excellent exposition), we've also added some lines to the parable of the prodigal son. They go something like this: "Father, I have come back to help You be more tolerant of the far country. In fact, I think some of the things I did in the far country should become part of our family life."

In the biblical account, the lines the prodigal rehearsed in the far country were very different than that and were based on his knowledge of the irreducible maximum of his father's authority. Whatever leniency he might receive, even being a hired servant instead of a son, would be his father's decision and more than he thought he deserved. So he said to himself, "I will arise and go to my father and I will say to him, 'Father, I have sinned against heaven and before you, and I am no longer worthy to be your son. Make me like one of your hired servants.' "

And when he saw his father running toward him and then felt his loving embrace, he made his confession because he already felt the father's forgiveness. If he hadn't known of both the strong integrity *and* the loving heart of his father, he probably would have stayed in the far country. It was because his father's household was distinctly different, that he wanted to come home.

When the Father is neglected in a congregation or denomination we will be diluted by cultural patterns, human values, moral proclivities, and sloppy subjectivism. We need God our Father, the God of holiness, goodness, and truth to reign supreme over the household of faith. When he does, divisions which pull us apart can be healed.

My survey of the expectations we have of the Congress indicates the need for that healing. All the varied emphases are rooted in the heart of the Father and it is there we meet each other and realize we can't exist for long without each other.

Paul's prayer for the Ephesians (Eph. 3:14–21) guides us in renewal as a Father movement. His prayer was made to ". . . the Father of our Lord Jesus Christ, from whom the whole family in heaven and earth is named . . ." (NKJV). It is the *pasa patria*, the whole family, that is our concern tonight. Paul prayed that the Ephesians be filled with the fullness of God. Why? So that the Father's glory would fill the whole church, not just one part or party, which might falsely think it is the whole. The Father's fullness is to produce a new oneness characterized by love and peace instead of strife and competition, by reconciliation instead of division and alienation, by unrelenting world evangelization instead of unremitting party spirit, and by battling evil and injustice in society instead of fighting for control in the church.

It's that fullness from the Father we are in danger of missing with our pride in pluralism and our elevation of eclecticism. Is that really as much of an achievement as we've touted? Is it maximum for ecclesiastics, evangelicals, charismatics, and mission-minded social activists to tolerate each other? Under the pleasantry of that toleration the old power struggles in the game of capture the flag are being played. Each group really wants the whole denomination to reflect its emphasis, goals, and language. We are delighted when one of our own particular group is recognized or elected to a key office. "There's hope for the denomination!" we shout with triumph. And so the political maneuvering goes on. We are no different than any humanly motivated political or governmental organization. And what's worse, we are like most of the other denominations.

The most serious, however, is that all four emphases evident in contemporary Presbyterianism are inseparably a part of the Father's fullness. But one without the rest is borderline heresy. We are thankful for evangelicals with their emphasis on the Bible and winning people to Christ. We need the fire and freedom of the charismatics. Also, we need to be the mission-social activists with their concern for the suffering in the world. And we need the ordered structure of the denominationalists who love our heritage and form of government. But we need something more. We need to incorporate all four emphases in a quadraphonic gospel. The four are never separated in the Father's heart. A lasting renewal that's a part of a Father movement will produce evangelical, Spirit-filled, socially relevant, committed church men and women.

Evangelicals with their emphasis on the Bible and the lordship of Christ need the fire and enthusiasm of the charismatics. The charismatics need to rediscover that the Holy Spirit is not a separate power to be possessed independent of the sovereignty of the Father and lordship of Christ. That produces pride and exclusivism. At the same time, the mission-minded, committed to changing society and meeting the suffering of humanity, need the piety and power of both the evangelicals and the charismatics if we are to avoid human burnout. And the faithful church men and women with deep commitment to the institutional church need to recognize that power comes from the Father and not our heritage, our structured procedures, or even our carefully-worded pronouncements.

Frankly, I don't want to try to make it without a wholeness which combines all of these emphases. All are part of the *telos* of the Father. I long to be part of a Father movement in which my "Abba Father" makes me open to an evangelical enthusiasm, a charismatic excitement, a mission-minded concern and a denominational loyalty.

It is because we have neglected the Father that we seek the human security of our separate groups. We gravitate to those who speak our language. We hover in unholy huddles. That even happens at a gathering like this. We seek out our own groups and look suspiciously at others. That results in the intensification of struggles for control.

The Father has brought us together to help us face our denial of his sovereign control of the church. He has brought this problem to the surface because he's ready to solve it. And he doesn't give up. He will continue to goad, challenge, and unsettle us until we submit to his authority. And what's most disturbing of all, he will withhold his blessings on our denomination until we humble ourselves and confess the diminutive gods we have made of our separate groups. And that must begin here at this Congress.

Only then will we be able to go back to our local churches to lead a Father renewal. It is sad that congregations become identified with one of the four emphases without the fullness of the Father's wholeness. We think of particular churches as evangelical, charismatic, socially activistic, or traditionally "Presbyterian" congregations. There are so few that are firmly balanced on the quadrapod of all four. And why? Why deify pluralism and eclecticism in congregations as a simplistic and irresponsible way of tolerating differences?

The most dynamic growing Presbyterian congregations in America have pulled out all four stops. Under the sovereignty of the Father, the Bible is being expounded with contemporary verve and vitality. There is both chrism and charismata, the anointing of the Spirit and the outpouring of the gifts for ministry. These congregations are distinguished for their strong involvement in suffering and giving to missions. And they are deeply committed to sharing in the connectional loyalties of the greater church. Why should we expect less of any local church?

Our churches are filled with people who are far more ready for a Father-guided renewal than we've dared to imagine. And what they will receive in our leadership when we return is dependent on what happens to us here together. Only what happens to us can happen through us! Only what's freshly rediscovered can be reproduced.

The fullness the Father offers will be realized only as we repent of our pride and satisfaction with what we are and have.

We need to claim all that is offered by the Father tonight.

His promise through Obadiah grips us impellingly, "But on Mount Zion there shall be deliverance, and there shall be holiness; the house of Jacob shall possess their possessions. The house of Jacob shall be a fire . . ." (Obad. 17,18 NKJV). The Father has delivered us on Calvary. He calls for a new holiness, a new assurance that we are his called and cherished saints belonging first and only to him. Then we can possess our possessions, and claim the fullness that is offered by the gracious, generous heart of the Father. "All things are yours," says Paul, ". . . the world or life or death, or things present or things to come—all are yours. And you are Christ's, and Christ is God's" (1 Cor. 3:21–23 NKJV).

I have a friend in Edinburgh, Scotland who correctly diagnoses a spiritual ailment I suffer from at times. "Lloyd, you're a stingy receiver!" He's right—so often I'm satisfied with far too little when the Father has so much more to give. I sense many of you share that problem. Repentance of that opens the floodgates for the Father's renewal. Renewal is simply receiving all the Father wants to give. And it's always more than we can imagine.

The gifts of the Father

Last Christmas a woman told me about a conflict between her husband and her son over a piece of property. The valuable land had been placed in the father's will for him, but the son wanted it now. When his father resisted his demands, a broken relationship resulted. The son seldom came home and kept an aloof distance from his father when he did visit. His mother told me that she had convinced her son to spend Christmas at home.

With grief she described the time of exchanging gifts on Christmas Eve. Her son opened all his presents except the one from his father. It was a tie-shaped box carefully wrapped with a card saying, "To my beloved son—Dad." The box was never opened. It remained under the tree unopened all Christmas day and the next, when the son left. What the young man did not know was that the father had neatly folded the deed of the property and placed it in the box as his Christmas gift to his son. And to this day the box is unopened. The land now belongs to the son, but he doesn't know it because he refused to unwrap the gift!

This Congress is our time to open our Heavenly Father's gifts. But in this case he offers them through us to each other and that means swallowing our pride and realizing that we need each other. The *metanoia*, the repentance, that is required tonight involves two turns: a turning around to meet the Father and then allowing him to turn us to each other to accept the gifts he offers us through each other.

A call for repentance as an admonition to ourselves and our peers in church leadership is not easy to give or to receive. Recently at the conclusion of a worship service in our church in Hollywood I walked up the aisle greeting people. Suddenly a young man stood in my path and would not allow me to pass. He had a grim, angry look on his face and blocked my steps by standing toe to toe, nose to nose. It was impossible to get around him, whatever way I tried.

"You must repent!" he said imperiously. Shocked by both his attitude and words, I asked him to let me pass and promised to talk with him after I finished greeting the people. Still blocking my every effort to move up the aisle, he repeated his fiery demand that I repent. Meanwhile, the congregation sat watching with stunned silence.

A third time, now with growing zeal, the man called for my repentance. This time he added, "You must give up your pride and repent!"

Looking him squarely in the eye I said, "I have and I will. Now let me pass." Finally he turned on his heel and walked out of the sanctuary and disappeared. I've never seen him since. I was left to wonder whether he was an angel sent to wrestle with a Jacob called Lloyd or a religious fanatic who thought he was the reincarnation of John the Baptist. It's not really important for me to decide. What is important is my daily, hourly need to give up false pride and repent of how little of the abundance of the generosity of the Father I've been willing to receive. And that call for repentance sounds in my soul with Fatherly authority and love most all of the time.

It is interesting as well as encouraging to note that in Luke's account of the Sermon on the Mount, he records that Jesus concluded the section of his messages on emulating the Father's generous heart with a mirthful metaphor rather than the words "You shall be perfect, just as your Father in heaven is perfect."

The metaphor thunders a salient truth. The Father has so much more to give than we have been willing to receive. "Give, and it will be given to you: good measure, pressed down, shaken together, and running over will be put into your bosom. For with the same measure that you use, it will be measured back to you" (Luke 6:38 NKJV). The picture is of a joyous Master rewarding his servants for their labors at harvest time. They had taken the seeds he had given them months before, and working side by side with the master, they had planted, cultivated, and with faithful labor had harvested the grain. Now the master knew no limits to his generous affirmation of his servants. He could not give them enough to express his delight in them.

Do we want renewal?

Something like that must have prompted Jesus' metaphor of overflowing blessings. It is the same exciting theme as the promise that it is the Father's purpose to help us accomplish our purpose. Renewal is really offering our empty bushel measures to receive a pressed down, overflowing abundance of the Father's blessing.

But do we want it? The question Jesus asked the paralyzed man at the pool of Bethesda is now the question before us as individuals and as a denomination. "Do you want to be made well?" (John 5:6). Like the man there at the pool we offer our excuses and try to place blame. These are swept aside and again we are confronted with our own spiritual impotence and the paralysis of the church in these late days of the twentieth century. We feel acutely our brokenness and need of healing.

I've often reflected on why John, in recording this miracle at the pool, made so much of the fact that the man had lingered by the pool for thirty-eight years without being healed. We remember the account of the people of Israel actually leaving Sinai. It makes the length of Israel's wandering in the wilderness total thirty-eight years.

Careful study of the Gospel of John reveals that the apostle often had two purposes in mind when he recorded the miracles of Jesus. He wanted to recount what happened and then drive home the deeper implication. We wonder if for John this paralytic was symbolic of Israel's spiritual paralysis in being unwilling to claim the promised land. The thirty-eight years of wandering back and forth in the wilderness wasn't because the Lord was unwilling to fulfill his promise, but because the people were reluctant to trust him. That same reluctance reoccurred throughout Israel's history and was expressed most tragically in the rejection of the Father's gift of the Messiah.

This miracle—the healing of the paralyzed man—has pointed application for religious institutions. Congregations, denominations, and spiritual leaders like you and I need to be asked repeatedly, "Do you want to be made well?" Admitting that we are ill and need healing is often difficult. Pride again. But when we do admit our need, the Father's healing is available.

What in your life needs healing? Hurting memories, failures, broken relationships, physical illness? And what about your congregation? In the opening hours of the Congress I visited with so many of you who are feeling frustration and discouragement over your churches. Others of you with whom I've talked are gripped by the "magnificent obsession" of your vision of your church truly coming alive and pressing forward in contagious evangelism and bold mission. And then what of our beloved denomination? Where are we going? Will union bring unity, will restructuring bring revival? And then we realize that what our denomination needs is exactly what this Congress needs: the Father's healing, an outpouring of his Spirit, a rejuvenated exuberance in all of us.

But healing, like our conversion, requires death before there is resurrection. And that death comes only through a complete surrender of ourselves with all our impotence and paralysis. Put another way, it means the relinquishment of ourselves, our congregations, and our denomination to the sovereignty of the Father. Judgment has begun here in the household of God. We're ill and need healing.

When Jesus reflected on the healing of the man by the pool, He said, "I made a man completely well" (John 7:23 NKJV). The Greek really means, "I made a whole man whole." May that be true for all of us tonight. But may it also be, "I made a whole Congress whole. And what I did there, is the beginning of what I will do in the whole denomination." And we cry out "Abba Father! Your will, not ours, be done!"

Last summer when I was in Edinburgh, Scotland I stayed in a hotel near New College where I took my study leave. One night I worked until dawn to finish a writing project. The light from my study lamp spilled out through the transom of the door into the corridor. When Kathy, a cheery elderly maid who has dyed carrot red hair and is as wide as she is tall, saw the light from my room she rapped gently at my door. I must have looked tired after a long night's work.

"Oh, Dr. Ogilvie," she said, "are ya still up? All this work is goin' to be the death o' ye." I smiled and told her I had to finish before going home.

"Have ye had yer breakfast?" she said, expressing her concern the best way she knew how. Suddenly I realized how hungry I'd become and agreed that some breakfast would be very nice. Just as she turned to go, she said, "And have ye heard God singin' yet this mornin'?"

I hadn't. I'd been too busy working for him to listen for his singing!

"It's in the Good Book ya know," Kathy said joyfully. "Yer supposed to be a scholar and should know where it is. Look it up while I fix yer breakfast!"

I returned to my desk and leafed through my Bible. Then I remembered where it was. I turned to Zephaniah 3:16, 17. "In that day it shall be said to Jerusalem: 'Do not fear; Zion, let not your hands be weak, the Lord your God in your midst, the Mighty One, will save; He will rejoice over you with gladness, He will quiet you in His love, He will rejoice over you with singing' " (NKJV).

In the quiet of early morning I heard God's song with the ears of my inner being. It was a song reminding me that he is in control, that he would accomplish his purpose in me and that his love would never fail. I'll never forget that song. It made my day, in fact, all of this past year.

Do you hear the Lord singing over you, over our church? His song reminds us there are four things we'll never have to do again. We don't have to question our worth to the Father. He loves us. We don't have to condemn or justify ourselves. We are his children, now and forever, through our exoneration and adoption through the Cross. We don't have to stay as we are. The Father's overflowing blessing has barely begun. And we don't have to run the church and assure its future on our own. The Father is in control. He created us in his image. There's no need to return the compliment!

The song the Father is singing tonight also includes an invitation. "I love you. Come home!"

My friend Charles Allen tells how his dad would come to watch and cheer when he played baseball as a boy. When he got a good hit and was running the bases, as he would round third base, his dad would shout, "Come home, Charles, come all the way home!"

That's what the Father God is saying to you and our denomination. "Come home, O dear Presbyterian family, come all the way home!"

And the Father-shaped void inside us responds. We need the Father. His majesty and glory. His holiness and healing. His judgment and grace. His everlasting arms!

As I close this evening's meeting I want you to place your hands in front of you. In one hand place the deepest need, the most urgent hope, the greatest vision you have right now. And then in the other hand place your convictions about God our Father. Don't leave anything out. Think of all he is and has done for you. Providential care. Cherishing love. The Cross. The power of the Resurrection. Pentecost. The fullness of the Spirit. Gifts for ministry. Open doors. A new beginning. All power in heaven and earth. The glory and majesty of God the Father!

Now, when you are ready, bring your hands together and claim all that is yours from the Father. Surrender your life to his sovereign authority. Say "Abba Father! Your will be done."

Having done that, take ahold of the hand of a person near you. Hold his or her hand up in affirmation of your desire to move beyond the security of whatever separate group in the church you've been a part. Confess the church's brokenness and divisions. Ask the Father to begin healing the church with the two of you.

Finally, in expression of your commitment to oneness in the Father, hold each other's hands high as you say together, "We belong to the Father and each other and claim him Lord of all! Hallelujah and amen."

5

RENEWAL AMIDST THE DARKNESS
Roberta Hestenes

Roberta Louis Hestenes is instructor in communication
and educational ministries at Fuller Theological Seminary,
Pasadena, California.

God, the Father, has rescued us from the dominion of darkness and brought us into the kingdom of the Son he loves, in whom we have redemption, the forgiveness of sins. Col. 1:13, 14 NIV

For you know that it was not with perishable things such as silver or gold that you were redeemed from the empty way of life handed down to you from your forefathers, but with the precious blood of Christ, a lamb without blemish or defect.

1 Pet. 1:18, 19 NIV

What does it mean to say that we have been rescued from the dominion of darkness and brought into the kingdom of the Son? What does it mean to say that Christ, the very lamb of God, the sinless one, is the Redeemer? Sometimes it seems too simple and too easy.

Redemption seems so clear and easy as I sit in comfortable American pews and sing with my fellow Christians. "Redeemed how I love to proclaim it! . . . Redeemed by the blood of the Lamb." The dark places and difficult passages of life—those in which we discover that God is not against us but for us—they seem far away. We can sing with joy and we can affirm with clarity: We have been rescued.

But the flies on the faces of the children in Ethiopia are not easy to look at. When I was there I kept wanting to reach out and brush them away, at least those flies that rested on the eyelids. The children's eyes were so large for such small bodies. The mothers desperately sought to nurse but had nothing in their breasts. The fathers tried to carry their children but barely had strength to move themselves. What does it mean to say Christians have been rescued from the dominion of darkness in Ethiopia? That we bury them with crosses around their necks?

The question confronts us not only in Ethiopia, so far away. The boy in our town was only fourteen. His parents got a messy divorce and they were apart. It was his birthday and he waited all day for his dad to call. And his dad didn't. The boy was found, hanged, at the end of the day. What does it mean, we have been "rescued . . . from the dominion of darkness . . ."? The darkness remains very real.

She called me and said, "I can't believe it, I can't believe it." She was crying. "Thirty-five years," she said. "Thirty-five years. Five children. I can't believe it." What? Her husband had left. He was gone; it was over. We have been "rescued . . . from the dominion of darkness . . ." but the darkness is very real.

How do we live in a world like this? Renewal does not come through the shutting of our eyes to the reality of the world. When we keep our eyes open we know that reality has to do with a world that is deeply mired in the throes of suffering. It is a world that tries in many different ways to redeem itself: many schemes, many programs, many philosophies, many campaigns, many self-promoting leaders. "If we could just shape it right," we think. "If we could just redo it. If we could just pass this law." But still there remains darkness and brokenness.

Renewal, the redemption of Christ, is related to the reality of this lost world. It is true that when we are redeemed by the blood of the Lamb we are taken into a new realm of existence. But that realm, that kingdom, exists in the midst of this lost world.

Three images of the Christian church help me as I wrestle with the meaning of the new life that we have been given in Jesus Christ. They are images from the Scripture that the church has reappropriated again and again through the centuries. And when the church has recaptured these images of what it is now, as the redeemed community, it finds a freshness, obedience, and focus that makes true citizens of the kingdom. The three images are the Exodus, the race, and the vine and branches.

The image of the Exodus

The experience of the Exodus was the formative experience for the people of Israel. After it, the Israelites understood themselves as the people who had been delivered from oppression, brought out of bondage into freedom. That is who they were. Their sense of identity and purpose was rooted in the Exodus.

The Exodus experience has chapters to it, chapters that are followed beyond the Old Testament in the New. As the early Christians pondered the meaning of the Exodus for Israel, they saw that experience lived out again in Jesus, the fulfillment of Israel. And as they looked at their own lives as those who had been redeemed, they looked to the Exodus story to draw meaning and purpose for their lives.

What are the chapters of the Exodus story? First, oppression, injustice, and daily, grinding bondage. The first chapter is being treated unfairly and neglected. The surprising note in the chapter of oppression is that God wasn't primarily interested in what was going on in Pharaoh's palace. He was paying attention to the people that Pharaoh was using and abusing and didn't care about. And God heard their cry; God saw their suffering; God moved to act. Moses, who knew the Pharaoh's palace and his people's suffering, tried to bring liberation. He tried first of all by his own stand, striking the guard dead. But the injustice only heightened. Moses' blow did not bring about liberation.

The lesson of the chapter of oppression is that we cannot deliver ourselves. So the next chapter is the deliverance of God. We are totally dependent on the merciful action of God, who hears our cry and bends to our conditions. He cares about the lost, the marginalized, and those treated unjustly. He acts to deliver, and the deliveries come with the blood of the spotless Lamb. The Israelites were told to brush the blood of the lamb on their doorposts, and destruction would pass over them. They would be brought safely through. We Christians also know deliverance by blood—the blood of the Lamb; we are delivered by the sacrifice of Jesus Christ.

Celebration . . . and wilderness

After deliverance comes the next chapter: celebration, or having a party. Israel moved out and crossed the sea. Miriam and the women led the people in singing and dancing, a celebration of what God had done. Surely that is our response to liberation in Jesus Christ. Redemption means celebration. We were lost; we are found. We were in darkness; we know light. We have moved, and we celebrate.

The chapter following celebration is one I don't like. (I have a friend who always reads the last chapter of a book first. I think that is cheating. But she wants to find out how the book is going to end rather than wade her way through the middle.) In actual life, however, we can't skip the next chapter. It should be the Promised Land. I would like the story to read "oppression," "deliverance," "celebration," and "Promised Land." Isn't every day with Jesus sweeter than the day before? Yes, but also, no. Because the next chapter isn't the Promised Land.

The next chapter for Israel, for Jesus, for the church, and for us, is the wilderness. It is learning how to live in freedom. The lesson doesn't come automatically. The world around us has told us what we should value. Now we find that we need a new set of values.

And here we are in the wilderness. We would like it to be safer and tamer and nicer. But something happens to people when they get into the wilderness. They often fight with each other. They scramble for scarce resources. They vie for leadership.

The Apostle Paul (in 1 Corinthians 10) talked about some of the lessons of the wilderness. They are important today as well. Paul said all of the people ate the spiritual food and drank the spiritual drink from the rock that was Christ. But nevertheless, God was not pleased with most of them. These things happened as examples to keep us from setting our hearts on evil things, Paul wrote. How can you be delivered from oppression and not yet have your heart turned, to seek fully the things of God? Don't be idolaters. Don't commit sexual immorality. Don't test the Lord in unbelief. And do not grumble.

What about this matter of grumbling? Some translations speak of murmuring, which once made me picture the Israelites whispering to each other. But in the camp of Israel, in the midst of the wilderness, there was more than whispering going on. There were choices that had to be made in response to what was happening in the wilderness. On some days the Israelites weren't sure they were going to have enough food to eat and on some days they were thirsty. On some days all they could think about was the cucumbers of Egypt—oh, for the cucumbers of Egypt!

They complained about the leadership: "What are you doing, bringing us out here to die? Why did you get us into this mess anyway, God? Moses? Miriam?" And we might ask today, what's so bad about complaining? I hear a lot of it in the church. I go to my share of meetings. I ask, "How is it going?" And I hear the grumbling.

Week by week, month by month, long year by long year, the way in which the people chose to respond to the demands of the wilderness shaped their ability to believe in the promises of God. They said God would not provide and he always did. That is the lesson of the wilderness. We have everything we need in it. It may not always feel good, but we have everything we need. God provides. The Israelites said, "I don't like it. I am bored with it. Manna again?"

Like the Israelites, we grumble. We are so newly out of bondage and oppression that we don't know a new language. But that language is in the New Testament. There is a word that occurs again and again. It looks small and insignificant, but it turns out to be very important. It is "thankfulness." Be thankful to God. Have a heart of gratitude, a heart of appreciation, a heart that says, "Lord, I don't deserve anything but you have given so much."

Faithfulness instead of grumbling is the lesson of the wilderness. As simple as it is, I do not believe we will move forward in renewal until we learn to have a thing called spirit. We need an awareness of the reality that there is Someone to be thankful to, Someone who is acting and alive and working in us and through us, moving us from the realm of darkness into the kingdom of his Son.

The image of the race

The second image of renewal: the race. Paul writes of running the race to win the prize, the crown that will last forever (1 Cor. 9:25). Hebrews 12:1 and 2 exhort us to run the race looking to Jesus, the "author" or "perfecter" of our faith. If the image of the Exodus speaks to us of testing and trusting, the image of the race speaks to us of disciplined movement toward the goal. Protestants, who have been brought up on justification by faith and the importance of grace, sometimes get nervous when there is talk about discipline in the Christian life. Yet there is discipline, focused in a direction which takes us toward the goal in front of us.

The importance of disciplined movement can be

understood when we consider the difference between pilgrims and gypsies. Pilgrims are people who are moving forward and know where they are going. They have a destination. Gypsies are people who like to move for the sake of moving. They spend time going to the same places again and again. The issue for us in the church is: Are we pilgrims or gypsies? Are we moving forward toward the goal of knowing Christ and being agents of his kingdom? Or are we just going over the same ground again and again?

The race we must run is not the rat race. It is not getting on the treadmill in the morning and meeting hourly appointments that will tell us that we have an identity. We try to find identity that way: "Look how important I must be, I don't have a minute today. You can't see me for five years on the second Tuesday of July." And the rat race becomes our race.

Hamsters in cages run the rat race. They get in their wheels and run nine thousand miles, but never get anywhere. And it can be like that in the church: endless committee meetings and activities, routines and procedures that we do over and over. They may have value, but have become for us a rat race to the point that we forget the goal.

A haunting analogy of this misdirected running can be drawn from the 1984 Olympics. A female marathon runner came into the arena with all her energy and strength depleted. As she staggered into the arena it was obvious that she was on automatic pilot. The legs were pumping simply because in the past they had been taught to pump. But her eyes were glazed over and she didn't know where the finish line was. Sometimes it is the same in the church. We forget our resources, we lose sight of the finish line, the goal toward which we run. We do have a race to run,

but it is not a short sprint. It calls for long-term persever-
ance. We won't reach the goal of knowing Christ without
disciplined effort.

The image of the vine and branches

The final image is that of the vine and branches. Jesus
said, "I am the true vine and my Father is the gardener.
He cuts off every branch in me that bears no fruit, while
every branch that does bear fruit he trims clean so that
it will be even more fruitful. . . . Remain in me, and I
will remain in you. No branch can bear fruit by itself; it
must remain in the vine. Neither can you bear fruit unless
you remain in me" (John 15:1–4 NIV). Is it true that we
can do nothing, bear no fruit, without Jesus?

One Sunday I was guest speaker at a church. When I
arrived, the head usher handed me the bulletin and said,
"You do everything."

"What?" I asked.

"You do everything. It's up to you to lead the worship."

There are some things we can do by ourselves. We can
have another committee meeting. We can conduct an order
of worship. But apart from Jesus we will not bear fruit.
There is a world that needs to know that Christ is the
Redeemer, that there is a kingdom of light, that goodness,
truth, and love exist and are powerful. But we are inade-
quate to the task of this telling and this witness. Just as
we could not redeem ourselves, neither can we be fruitful
ourselves.

Elton Trueblood wrote of the dangers of a cut-flower
civilization, a civilization that wanted the benefits of the
Christian faith without believing in the Christian faith. A
cut-flower civilization wanted the character, the hard work,
the morality, the ethic of Christianity without wanting to

have its roots in Jesus Christ, the Lamb of God who alone can nourish these flowers.

We must beware lest we have a cut-flower church, a church that wants the fruits of Christian faith but does not want to go deep in the life of prayer. We must go deep in our dependence upon God so that his life and power flow through us. Only then can we make a difference in the real world.

The images together

These are the three images: we are called as an Exodus people, redeemed by the blood of Christ, traveling light through the wilderness. We are a disciplined people, controlled by the vision of Christ, racing toward him as our goal. We are also people rooted in God, bearing fruit only in dependence on him, and bearing it in a hurting, needy world. What does it mean to be redeemed? It means that we are part of the adventure of what God is doing in the world. There is no more exciting life than that.

6

THE PERSON AND WORK OF JESUS CHRIST
Cecilio Arrastia

Dr. Cecilio Arrastia is Associate for Developing Resources and Services, Presbyterian Evangelism Program, Presbyterian Church (USA), with offices in New York, New York.

WHO IS JESUS CHRIST?

That is a question that can be phrased in four short words. But it is a profound question. Jesus, the Christ, stands at the very center of the Christian proclamation. The name, the person, and the work of Christ are essential to the Christian outlook. He is not simply a "starting point" or a "sparkplug" in the Christian experience. He is the locus of God's encounter with his creation. What we know of God we know through him. What we know of ourselves we know through him. We cannot think with intelligence of God and humanity without Christ in our thinking.

And the more we think in these terms, the clearer it

becomes to us. The basic declaration about Christ is this: Jesus is Lord. In other words, he bears the marks of God's own personality. He has never been equaled as a man because he is more than a human possibility.

The fascinating and mysterious reality is that this Lord comes to us in three key events which proclaim not only his power but also his humility, his willingness to deny himself. These key events are the Incarnation, the Crucifixion, and the Resurrection.

The first mystery is that of the Incarnation. "In the beginning was the Word, and the Word was with God, and the Word was God" (John 1:1). And this Word became flesh and lived among us, so that we could see his glory. All this was done because God was working in Christ to bring about reconciliation with the world (2 Cor. 5:19). There is a flow of actions that starts with God's purpose, moves through the birth at Bethlehem, and goes all the way to Calvary.

At Calvary is found the second mystery, the Crucifixion of the Word made flesh. If the Incarnation is, as Gustaf Aulén has said, the necessary preliminary atoning work, then the Cross becomes the necessary intermediate step. Christ's humanity—his incarnation—was followed by his crucifixion. Christ died to justify human beings before God, to make us holy, to eliminate our guilt. Whatever theory of atonement is stressed—ransom, sacrifice, reconciliation, or even *Christus Victor*—the central fact does not change: Christ died in obedience to God's project to save persons.

And when we inject the concept of victory into these reflections, we must turn to the third mystery of our faith, the Resurrection of Christ. This proclamation of the glory and joy of the Resurrection lies at the heart of the basic

Christian outline. As Scripture puts it, "If Christ has not been raised, then our preaching is in vain and your faith is in vain" (1 Cor. 15:14 RSV).

The Resurrection is a vindication of God. God's integrity and character are at stake when Christ hangs from the cross. The Resurrection is the beginning of a new creation in which God's character is validated and documented—God cares; he did not abandon his Son or his people. The Resurrection is also a vindication of Christ's person and his work. It proves that his followers had not misplaced their trust. His resurrection brought about the resurrection of his followers; their joy came back to life. The depression of his death was gone. "The Lord is risen" is the proclamation of a personal victory. "See, I told you so," the disciples seem to say. "Our hopes were not in vain." Their submission to Rome, to Israel, was finished. Exodus II took place. They had crossed another Red Sea—led by Christ, a second and greater Moses. They were a free community.

The power of the Incarnation

Yet how can we say that the disciples' submission to Rome or to Israel was affected by Christ's Incarnation, Cross, and Resurrection? Does Christ's person and work somehow affect politics, religion, nature, and the rest of existence?

The inclusive and universal character of Jesus' person and work are reflected in the titles he bore in the Bible: Prophet, High Priest, Mediator, Servant of God, Lamb of God, Messiah, Son of David, Son of Man, Judge, Holy One of God, Savior, King, Logos, Son of God, Lord and God.

A whole constellation of meanings are hidden in these titles. The worlds of politics, religion, nature, reason, legal advocacy, messianic hope, and sacrificial rites are covered or touched by these titles. But the fascinating reality, according to theologian Oscar Cullman, is that no single one of these titles fully explains, describes, or reveals the totality of Christ's person and ministry. Only taken together do they describe all the components of his work: his preexistence, his earthly ministry, his present work, his future work. Both the beginning of time and the consummation of time, the Alpha and the Omega of history, are represented in these titles. No wonder the Bible says that Jesus Christ is the only name given to humanity through which we can reach salvation.

The common denominator of these many titles is their revelatory character. This revelation has a paradoxical character. On the one hand, Christ reveals the nearness of God, his radical tenderness and compassion. On the other hand, Christ reveals—through his integrity, holiness, and radical obedience—the distance that exists between God and his creation.

Christ is God near us, around us, in us, and for us. His arms embrace us and protect us. He is Emmanuel—God with us. But he is also God far away from us. He reveals our sinful intentions which lead to alienation and death. While he affirms God for us, he also reveals a human race opposed to him, running away from the "heavenly hound" of Francis Thompson.

In other words, Christ is the way to human despair, but also the only way out of despair to hope and salvation. It has been said that it is dangerous to know God without knowing our own misery; but it is also dangerous to know our own misery without knowing God. The first option brings about false pride and olympic arrogance; the second brings about cynicism and frustration, with a tragic sense of life. Christ takes care of our despair because he reveals both God's love and our own misery. He sank to the deepest of all loneliness when he cried, "My God, my God, why hast thou forsaken me?" (Mark 15:34), but he ascended to the highest of all peace and tranquility when he said "Father, into thy hands I commend my spirit" (Luke 23:46).

Therefore, neither false pride nor depression exist in the lives of those whose hearts have been invaded by Christ's light and life.

But who is Christ for us?

In speaking of human hearts, we come to a basic reality. The answer to our central question—who is Christ?—cannot be found in merely academic, contemplative fashion. It cannot be found unless something is added: Who is Christ *for us*? In other words, only when we face him in a personal way and stop playing with ideas about him will we be able to discern the truth and be discovered by the Christ. We can look for a redeeming answer in all the creeds and confessions of the church—Nicene, Apostolic, Chalcedonian, Scots, Second Helvetic Confession, or any others—and the question will still haunt us: Who is Jesus Christ for me, for you, for us? In the renewal of our private personal world, in the renewal of our universe of priorities, values, and dreams, in the renewal of his mystical body the church, in the renewal of a world of misery and anxiety—who is Christ?

A well-known biblical incident illuminates this issue.

The moment was a private one between the Master and his disciples. Two questions were lingering in Jesus' mind. First, the introductory one: "Who do men say that I, the Son of man, am?" (Matt. 16:13.) All answers pointed to the past: John the Baptist, Elijah, Jeremiah—all persons of history gone by, all of them dead. It would be great for his enemies if Christ could be limited to the past or if he were simply dead. It is always easier to deal with the past than with the future. And it is easier to deal with a dead body than to struggle with one that is alive and powerful. To exile Christ to a meaningless past would mean the elimination of all the threats that he poses to our lifestyle, of all the commands that he presents to us. To bury him and forget even the location of his burial place would be to "recover" paradise, at least for those who are his enemies.

But this first question—who do *they* say I am?—is merely a pretext to get to the real one. The real question is this: "Who do *you* say I am?" (v. 15 NEB, italics added). This is the question that can lead to renewal. Renewal begins— or ends—with the answer we give to this question. In this case, Peter's prophetic reply is clear: "You are the Messiah, the Son of the living God" (Matt. 16:16 NEB). Peter's remarks are eloquent: This truth is a revealed one; it comes down from heaven; it is given to us by God's grace. Moreover, it has transforming power. To know this will mean a new life, a new beginning.

There is something else to Peter's answer. Implicit in it is this: When we answer the question about who Christ is, we are also answering the question about our own being—who we are. We know who we are when we know ourselves in and through the person and work of Christ. Our identity is not defined by fame, intelligence, or personal charisma, but by humble service to others in the name of Christ.

If you have any doubt, listen to the rest of the story. "And I say this to you: You are Peter, the Rock; and on this rock I will build my church, . . ." (Matt. 16:18 NEB). The new nature of a formerly weak and hesitant Peter is revealed and defined. Apart from Christ we are faceless, nameless, confused people—invisible men and women, without hope or destiny. It is the role of Christ's person and work to help us to define our own humanity and our final destiny. In him we become, like Peter, rocks upon which the church can be built and renewed.

Our personal and institutional renewal are related to the nature of our answer, to our personal, private, intimate—but *public*—answer to this question: Who is Christ, for *us*?

What Jesus reveals: two biblical vignettes

Let us suppose that we have answered the question properly. Christ is, we say, Messiah, Son of God, Lord, God! Another question, however, immediately arises. What kind of a Lord, what kind of a God? If Christ is an instrument of revelation, what exactly does he reveal? If he is the only true, full, authentic human being, what kind of humanity does he incarnate? What does his person and work tell us about his inner being?

Once again, consider two biblical vignettes.

Vignette Number One: "As he saw the crowds, his heart was filled with pity for them, because they were worried and helpless, like sheep without a shepherd" (Matt. 9:36 TEV). Beggars, cripples, lepers, blind people—marginal, oppressed people, undocumented, victims of both a tyrannic government and a legalistic religious system—not merely sinful people, but victims living without connection to their heavenly Father, with the anxiety and the fear of a lamb without a shepherd.

Looking at these people, Jesus felt pity, compassion,

love. He was the incarnation of genuine *agape*—for he loved those who did not deserve love, those who were repulsive to the eye and the nose. Here we are dealing with Christ's person, with the intrinsic nature of his being. He is love as God is love. Nothing human is alien to him—pain, frustration, slavery, oppression. To the victims of alcoholism and drug abuse; to those who suffer as the result of racial, economic, or cultural discrimination; to women, very often despised and ignored because of their sex; to all these he speaks: "God loves you. Rejoice because yours is the kingdom of heaven."

And he proclaims this message without articulating a single word, just by being what he is; by the miracle of his person. In him love is not an accident. It is a constant, permanent, functional reality that provides the basis for all that he does. For many leaders of the world, leaders of revolutions that later betray their people, love is just an accidental appendix. But Christ came to lead the blind and to make whole the broken ones, because he is love, as "God is love" (1 John 4:8).

In English we have the word *pity*. It points to our compassion for others. A Latin word, *pietas*, points to God, to our sense of devotion and nothingness in facing his holiness and integrity.

We human beings very often tend to separate these two feelings, and we pretend to feel pity without *pietas*. Or we exhibit our *pietas* without showing any sense of pity. In Christ's person and work these two elements always traveled together. His *pietas* or love of God allowed him to feel pity for others; and when he faced the pain and the plight of others, it was his *pietas* that was the source of his power and compassion.

Jesus was not a person who was moved but then did

nothing. Because of his love "Jesus went round all the towns and villages teaching in their synagogues, announcing the good news of the Kingdom, and curing every kind of ailment and disease" (Matt. 9:35 NEB). This points to his work—to what comes out as a result of his inner being. And here we see a redeeming flow between his person and his work. It is in this context, more than in the area of speculation and abstract thinking, that we see the divine and the human at work in Christ.

If we try to apply these dynamics to renewal, we will see that here there is a starting point. First, we have to deal with our own personhood, our own inner being. We have to confront all our distortions with God's sanctity. We have to be radicals, going to the roots of our selfishness and allowing the power of Christ to work in us.

Having done this, we must engage ourselves in a liberating struggle for others—teaching, proclaiming, healing, casting out demons that threaten to destroy the souls of our cities and communities. In the interaction of our person and our work renewal will become a reality in the life of the church. In other words, Christ is the model *par excellence.*

Vignette Number Two: A rich young man asked Jesus, "Teacher, what good thing must I do to receive eternal life?" Jesus replied, " 'If you want to be perfect [complete], go and sell all you have and give the money to the poor, and you will have riches in heaven; then come and follow me' " (Matt. 19:16, 21 TEV). Another question: "How can a man be born when he [or she] is old?" (John 3:4). And the answer: "Except a man be born of water and of the Spirit, he [or she] cannot enter into the kingdom of God" (John 3:5).

In these two incidents we find Jesus dealing with rich,

powerful men. The same Christ who was concerned and felt pity for the poor and the oppressed now provides a formula for these two rich men, whom he loves, to enter into the kingdom. The Christ of the gospel, then, is not *only* the Christ of the poor. Being a cosmic Christ, with love for all creation, he is also interested in the liberation and the salvation of those who are powerful and rich.

Christ knew very well that the liberation of the poor does not have a lasting effect unless the rich and the oppressor are also liberated. He knew human nature and he knew that very often the so-called liberator becomes the new oppressor. Unless there is a personal transformation in the new liberator, he or she will soon become an oppressor just like the one destroyed in the revolutionary project.

In other words, to limit the salvific power of the gospel to one social class is to reduce the scope and the possibilities of the gospel. It is to betray the universal dream of the Lord and practice some form of reductionism in dealing with the person and work of Christ. This would make the gospel a unilateral, populist, demagogic message. God's final goal in history has to be the liberation and salvation of all: the rich and poor, the weak and the powerful, men and women, all races and colors. If we proclaim the fact that God's concern is a total one that includes love for everybody, then the church will be the instrument to proclaim a gospel that might bring *shalom* for all of God's creation—not only for a social or economic class.

There is one aspect of Christ's person and work that we have to underline. In order to guarantee the integrity of both his person and his work, the Lord never made a compromise—neither with the substance of his proclamation nor with the language that he used to proclaim his message. He did not make a secret covenant with the religious, political, and military leaders of his time in order to advance his kingdom. He exhibited always an undivided loyalty to the Father that was the center of his message and life. He did not appeal to concessions that, in the long run, could contaminate the essence of his ministry. He could have lowered the standards of discipleship when talking to the rich young ruler or to Nicodemus, but he did not. Christ's loyalty to God implied a nonnegotiable integrity, both in work and deed.

It is not always so with us. In early November of 1984, the bishops of the Roman Catholic Church published a document dealing with poverty and affluence in this country. A loyal Roman Catholic layman, a journalist writing for the *New York Daily News*, published an interesting reaction to that document. The heart of his reaction was that there is an abyss between the words of the bishops and the way they live.

"People," he said, "would rather see a sermon than hear one, so Catholic bishops should vacate their plush residences and convert them into shelters for the homeless." The writer affirms the need of spiritual leadership in the area of economics, on the basis that "the storing up of riches was anathema to Jesus." But he regrets the lack of credibility of the bishops in this respect because, he says, "from the Vatican on down, bishops have cooks, maids, housekeepers, secretaries, every personal convenience, the best medical coverage, practically unlimited personal funds. The shepherds are too remote from the flock."

And, we add, in this area lies the unique integrity of Christ. How far from the poor are not only the bishops, but many so-called "liberators" living in luxury, enjoying privileges of the elite, while those whom they are supposed to have liberated are still in hunger and poverty?

The truth that cannot be changed

D. T. Niles has written one thing that we cannot afford to forget. Jesus Christ is not a value that we can negotiate, he says, nor is he a preference that we can reject. He is the truth, and the truth cannot be changed.

But there is more. This truth tells us that God loves the world, and because he loves, this loving truth demands a decision on our part.

Christ does not come to us as a proposition that we can endlessly discuss. He does not come as a theological concept that we can enlarge or cut into pieces. He comes as a King demanding obedience and submission, as a Teacher demanding discipleship, as a Savior demanding confession, as a God demanding worship, and as a Lord looking for humble servants.

By answering his call we will find real renewal and participate in victory that Christ already has won for us, for after all, "The gospel is a call to a battle whose final victory is already won."

7
ONE IN THE SPIRIT
Melicent Huneycutt

Dr. Melicent Huneycutt is the associate pastor for education and spiritual growth in The First Presbyterian Church of Evanston, Evanston, Illinois.

IN TEXAS RECENTLY, I HEARD AN AGGIE JOKE. TWO AGGIES were walking along a railroad track one day when they came upon a human arm. "Looks like Joe's arm," said the first.

Examining it carefully, the second exclaimed, "It is Joe's arm!" and the two continued down the track. Soon they found a leg.

"Looks like Joe's leg."

"Hmmm. It *is* Joe's leg."

They walked on, and found a head.

"Looks like Joe's head."

"Hmmm. It *is* Joe's head." Bending over, the second

Aggie grasped the head by the ears, shook it, and cried, "Joe! Joe! Are you hurt?"

The tragedy of the broken body

The joke is funny, but it is tragic. It reminds me of the body of Christ. We walk down the railroad track of disputes, and we see cut off here a charismatic arm, there a genuine born-again leg. Farther down the track we discover a post-trib premillenarian hand and a social activist liberal foot. Finally we come to the head, and our heartfelt cry is, "Jesus! Jesus! Are you hurt?"

J. I. Packer has said that the greatest work of the Holy Spirit is flooding our hearts with the love of God, making us one with the Father, with the Son, and with one another. We become the here-and-now body of Christ because the Holy Spirit floods us with God's love.

How does this oneness in God's love come about?

The Holy Spirit convicts us of sin, showing us our brokenness and helplessness. We cannot, by our own power, become the free and healthy persons we were created to be.

The Holy Spirit convicts us of God's righteousness, showing us the radiant perfection of the Christ who came to rescue, redeem, and sanctify us.

And the Holy Spirit convicts us of judgment, showing us that our old selves can be judged, overcome, that we can "be like [Christ], for we shall see him as he is" (1 John 3:2).

The Spirit fills us with love for the Father because God first loved us and sent the Son. The Spirit fills us with love for the Son because he poured out himself to make life possible for us. The Spirit makes us want to be one with God.

One with God—I in God, you in God, we in God; I in Christ, you in Christ, we in Christ—surely then we are one with each other? We should share one heartbeat, breathe one breath, move in harmony as we respond together to the Spirit. But *this* body, unlike poor Joe's in the Aggie joke, can choose whether or not it is to be fragmented. And all too often it chooses to be broken. Because God has given us free will and that free will is fallen, our choice will seldom be mutual confession, forgiveness, listening, and support. The only way we will ever truly be one in the Spirit will be through spiritual renewal—individual renewal, yes, but even more dynamically, renewal together as the body of Christ.

How Jesus yearned, during his last hours on earth, for the renewal of his new body, the church! His first body was ready to be broken, ready to leave this earth and return to the Father. Reading John 13–17, we listen as Jesus pours out his heart, encouraging those who love him to understand their relationship to one another in him. Especially in the high priestly prayer of John 17, the words of Jesus vibrate with longing that his friends be renewed into an indescribable oneness, just as he and the Father are one. Three phrases in Jesus' prayer reveal his hope for us truly to become "one in the Spirit."

"For them I sanctify myself"

In the portion of his prayer recorded in John 17:13–19, Jesus beseeches the Father to protect his friends as he sends them into the world. They are not of the world even as he himself is not. For their sakes, Jesus is sanctifying himself—making himself holy, setting himself apart for God's special purposes. What a poignant moment that must have been for the disciples who were participating in that prayer! They had just been told, " 'One of you is going to betray me" (John 13:21 NIV). Jesus himself, soon to be crying out, "Take this cup from me," must have trembled with the immediacy of the sanctification he was choosing (Luke 22:42 NIV).

"Although he was a son, he learned obedience from what he suffered . . . ," said the writer of Hebrews, reflecting that, "In bringing many sons to glory, it was fitting that God . . . should make the author of their salvation perfect through suffering" (Heb. 5:8, 2:10 NIV). From the moment when Christ had emptied himself of heavenly glory in order to take on his earthly body, he had never faltered in the obedience that made him one with the Father, but had continually permitted the Holy Spirit to inform his thoughts, words, and actions. Now, facing the Cross, he pled with God that his friends would also be set aside, sanctified, made holy, and sent into the world even as he himself had been sent into the world.

What a prayer for us! That we might obey to our last breath as he obeyed, that we might let God so love the world through us that we should lay down our lives for those whom God loves, that we become "living sacrifices, holy and pleasing to God," always open through the Holy Spirit to live out the will of the Father (Rom. 12:1 NIV).

And it is a prayer for *us*. Though each of us desires to offer his or her individual body to express God's love, it is only as we learn to remain obedient together that we become effective in revealing the magnitude and beauty of God's love. It is our lives laid down together, under the Holy Spirit's coordinating grace, that become a flexible and useful expression of God's life in the world.

Suppose Jesus of Nazareth had been as handicapped in his first body as Christ is in his here-and-now body.

Suppose his arm and hand had been reluctant to reach out to touch the anguished leper. Suppose his tongue and throat had refused to respond to the words his brain poured out to them, so that he could only wrench out syllable by slow syllable. Suppose, instead of flexing to his every will with readiness and grace, that first body had resisted the coordinating force of the Holy Spirit, each member moving unmindful of all the others, some paralyzed and some spastic, and some with a life all their own. How would the world have known with any clarity the quality of love God was offering through the Son?

Sadly, we, the here-and-now body of Christ, are reluctant to be used in coordination with one another. We often fail to wait together for the life-pulse of the Holy Spirit that will move us in harmony. We often refuse the suffering of remaining together while the Holy Spirit perfects us, sanctifying us together to become a whole and healthy body.

In our fear, we pull apart from each other, fragmenting and breaking this body in a more maiming way than the first body was broken on the cross. Our fragmentation prevents the free and jubilant expression of God's love. Yet for that free and jubilant expression we were created as a body. We profoundly need the discipline of daring to work through our differences together, so that our feet upon the mountains may dance gracefully to the good news. Cutting off an uncoordinated foot is hardly preparation for the loveliest dancing.

"I pray . . . that all of them may be one, Father"

The second phrase we emphasize in Jesus' prayer displays his deep concern for his friends: "I pray . . . that all of them may be one, Father, . . . as we are one: I in them and you in me" (John 17:20–23 NIV). Because the Holy Spirit who indwells us is the Spirit of the risen Christ, Jesus himself is in each of us. Since each of us partakes in him, we become partakers in God, and partakers in one another.

A few minutes before he prayed this prayer, Jesus had broken bread for his friends, saying, "This is my body given for you; do this in remembrance of me" (Luke 22:19 NIV). He had poured a cup of wine and urged each of them to share in what Paul was later to call the cup of "participation in the blood of Christ" (1 Cor. 10:16 NIV). Participating in his body, participating in his blood, all of us share in one another.

Consider it. Each one of us who comes into the body of Christ comes in through his blood. Whether I am a charismatic or a liberal or a member of the Moral Majority or an old-time Presbyterian, if I am in Christ, I came in through the Cross. Only through the Cross am I personally renewed, my past of frustration and failure cleansed, my broken self restored. And because each of us has participated in the blood of Christ, we can trust each other. The middle wall of partition is broken down. You, a new person, can learn to be one with me, a new person, since we are both partakers in the same blood.

Similarly, participation in the bread is participation in Christ's body. Once we have together received bread broken from one loaf, we have become one loaf. Unless each one who has eaten reassembles, the loaf can never be brought together again. We are now partakers in his body through his Holy Spirit. Sharing the same Spirit, we are one, organically one. And the Spirit, partaking in each one of us, will move us in harmony with one another.

This, again, is Jesus' midnight prayer: "That all of them

may be one, Father, just as . . . we are one" (John 17:21, 23 NIV). He yearns that we may be one *just as* he and the Father are one. Yet Jesus and the Father are more intimately one than we can imagine. What does Jesus mean by such a prayer?

Indwelt by the Holy Spirit, we share in the nature of God. That means we will interact with one another when we permit the Spirit to live in us, just as the Father interacts with Jesus and Jesus interacts with the Father. We can learn about Jesus' desire for our life together by observing how he interacted with the Father.

For one thing, we see that the Father and Son rejoice in their differences as well as in their likenesses. Nowhere do we find the Father deploring the fact that the Son is so unspiritual as to sweat, to have emotions, or to get tired. In fact, God is delighted that Jesus is different, for to be physical is a gift given the Son for his ministry. On the other hand, Jesus never complains that God is too spiritual, too ethereal, too absolute. No, he loves the fact that the Father is different from his own humanness. He learns to work creatively because of the Father's creativeness, and the Father's omnipresence comforts and supports him in his weakness and weariness.

If we could delight in our differences as the Father and Son delight in theirs, understanding that differing gifts and differing insights give the whole body a larger ministry, we would save ourselves much pain. Our focus could then be on our mission to the hurting people of the world, not on judging one another or on measuring up to one another.

A second aspect of the holy relationship is expressed by Jesus as he tells the Father, "All I have is yours, and all you have is mine" (John 17:10 NIV). In the early days of the church, when people remembered Jesus and his ways, and understood the Spirit newly given to be quickening them to those ways, one of the dynamic witnesses to changed life was shared possessions. "All the believers were together and had everything in common," reports Luke. "No one claimed that any of his possessions was his own, but they shared everything they had" (Acts 2:44; 4:32 NIV).

A Spirit-filled person no longer may refer to anything as "mine." Everything is now "ours," for we are one *just as* the Father is one with the Son. No more than Jesus withheld anything from the Father, nor the Father anything from the Son, no more can we withhold from one another things that could bring life, health, or joy. Thus Paul could urge believers on one continent to supply the needs of those on another continent, "that there might be equality" (2 Cor. 8:13 NIV).

The oneness that expresses itself in this kind of practical love turned the first century world upside down. Observers were "filled with awe" (Acts 2:43 NIV). The church found favor with "all the people. And the Lord added to their number daily those who were being saved" (Acts 2:47 NIV). Filled with the same Spirit, we might also so love that we no longer consider ourselves as *giving* what is ours, but simply as *being* one in the Spirit. What a challenge to discover the terms in which we can express God's love to one another, to learn to say, "All that I have is yours"!

Called to be one body just as the Father was in the Son and the Son was in the Father, we are called to a radically sacrificial lifestyle. Warm fuzzies and pat answers are not even a beginning to the kind of tough togetherness Jesus pleads the Father to bring to us.

"May they be brought into complete unity . . ."

There is another point in the prayer that we should consider. Jesus confirms the almost incredible reason for his plea that we be one, even as he and the Father are one. Just as the Father sent him into the world, Jesus states, he is sending us into the world. For that reason he is sanctifying himself; and through his commitment and suffering, he asks that we "too may be truly sanctified" (John 17:19 NIV).

Jesus needed his first body so that people might see with their own eyes, hear with their own ears, and feel with their own hands the love and power of God. His body translated God's love into terms people could receive. His prayer indicates that he intends us, his here-and-now body, to be the same yielded, committed instrument for communicating the sacrificial and redemptive love of God. Seldom have bodies of believers held still while the Holy Spirit purged, purified, and sanctified them into such yieldedness. Generally we splinter under the pressure, each one going out into "my" ministry. We fail to find the oneness that would amaze the world into belief. Yet that amazing unity under stress is the very thing Christ seeks in us, for such an unexpected oneness will convince the world that God is at work in love.

Our oneness is meant to be the greatest testimony to the supernatural, redeeming power of God in Christ. The winsomeness of our loving community of faith witnesses to an uprooted world that God is love and that God is with us. A fragmented and mutually judgmental church witnesses only to the failure of the human spirit.

In today's mobile and changing society, folk feel a deep need for a stable and caring community. By becoming a community of heterogeneous believers knit together by one bond, the blood of Jesus applied by the Spirit, we will reach out with healing and comfort to the world for which Christ's first body was broken. "As the Father has sent me," Jesus seems to be saying, "so I am sending you, all of you, you together."

Jesus' first body had to be broken that God's love could be made manifest. The here-and-now body, animated by the Spirit, may choose not to be broken. To choose to love until we are made one is to choose wholeness for ourselves. More greatly, more marvelously, it is to choose a ministry of wholeness to the hurting world. Our wholeness is intended to become a model of the healing, restoring, unifying love of God in Christ, to whom be glory, honor, dominion, and power forever.

8
WHERE'S THE POWER?
Samuel Hugh Moffett

Dr. Samuel Hugh Moffett is the Henry Winters Luce Professor of Ecumenics and Mission at Princeton Theological Seminary, Princeton, New Jersey.

IN ACTS 1:8 IS RECORDED THE GREATEST OF ALL THE GREAT promises of God. Jesus is saying goodbye to his disciples before he is taken up from them into heaven. And he speaks these words: "You shall receive power when the Holy Spirit has come upon you; and you shall be my witnesses in Jerusalem and in all Judea and Samaria and to the end of the earth" (RSV).

"You shall receive power. . . ." Strictly speaking, of course, no one promise of God is greater than all the others. But to me this is the greatest because it is what I need most. As a Presbyterian, I have plenty of order and decency. But where's the power?

119

In Acts 1:8 is also recorded the greatest of all forms of the Great Commission. "You shall be my witnesses . . . to the end of the earth." There is a form of this commissioning in each of the four Gospels, but this one in the book of Acts is the greatest. Strictly speaking, again, no one form of God's commissioning is greater than any other. But to me this is the greatest because it is the one I need most, the one we all need most. We're all Presbyterian, with sentimental, upper middle-class virtues. And where's the power—the power to propel us out of our comfortable, isolated churches and across the world? Our members are leaving; our missions declining. If power is what God promises, isn't that just what we all need most?

The promise of power

It makes sense to begin with the promise of power— "You shall receive power. . . ." I'm not sure that the disciples really believed that promise. They were too much like us. They were about as unrenewed, powerless, unfocused and puzzled a group as we American Christians. And like contemporary American Presbyterians, they were losing members. A few days before they had been twelve. Now they were only eleven. That's even worse than Presbyterians. We lose forty thousand a year, one of every eighty. The disciples lost one out of twelve!

So, disturbed and anxious, they turned to Jesus. But the first question they asked was the wrong question. All they wanted to know was, "When does the revolution begin? When will you bring in the kingdom?" They were still thinking in political terms, which is all right in its place, but this was neither the place nor the time for the question, and Jesus turned them away. "This is not for you to know," he said. But because he loved them, he gave them a promise, a promise centered in a different kind of kingdom. "You shall receive power when the Holy Spirit has come . . . and you shall be my witnesses . . . to the end of the earth."

Then he left them—with many questions unanswered, still unrenewed, still puzzled, still powerless. But isn't that how renewal always begins, not with power for the ambitious and powerful, but with a promise of power for those who have never had power, or have lost it?

That is how it began in Korea, where I was on the mission field, and which is now celebrating one hundred years of Protestant Christianity. In some ways, those first Korean Christians weren't much to celebrate. One of the best of them was a converted saloon keeper, really only partly renewed. Another was a 27-year-old student of the Chinese classics who fancied himself a philosopher and whose greatest religious experience had been a dream of the moon rising in his stomach. Still another was wrestling with the awful secret that he had taken a second wife before he was converted, and could not bear to leave her. Like the disciples, they weren't much to boast about.

But the gospel is good news. It is grace for the sinful, not for those who think they have no sin. It is healing for the sick, release for captives, sight for the blind, peace for the troubled, justice for the downtrodden, renewal for empty hearts. And as at Jerusalem, it is power for the powerless.

Whether or not the disappointed little group of disciples believed the promise, when Jesus was just about to leave them, they did the right thing. They trudged back down the hill into the city and "with one accord devoted themselves to prayer, together with the women and Mary the mother of Jesus, and with his brothers" (Acts 1:14 RSV).

They gave themselves to prayer. Weren't there more important things to engage the attention of serious men and women that day? There was news that the German barbarians were again raiding across the Rhine, news of a conspiracy against the life of Emperor Tiberius in Rome, and of a famine spreading across North Africa. Most people still think that those are the kinds of issues that really matter. And they do matter. But all the disciples did was go home and pray!

Prayer, says the secular world, is the Christian's escape from reality, a cop-out. Not long after my wife and I returned from missions work in Korea, one woman asked her, "What did you do for the people unjustly imprisoned by the government there?" It was a good question, and it was not asked unkindly. Eileen paused and answered, "There wasn't too much we could do. We visited them when we could. And we prayed for them regularly." That was when someone audibly whispered, "Cop-out."

I admit, there are times when I am more tempted to revolution than to prayer. And apparently it was revolution the disciples were thinking about when they asked Jesus, "Lord, will you at this time restore the kingdom to Israel?" But remembering how Jesus had answered them, they prayed instead of revolting.

Here is the paradox. Revolutions make the headlines. Prayer doesn't. But the world has forgotten about the plot against Tiberius that set tongues wagging in Jerusalem. It has forgotten the border raids across the Rhine. What it has never forgotten is that leaderless, outcast little band that trudged down the hill into Jerusalem—and took the time to pray.

There was a time in Korea when missionaries and Korean Christians were so discouraged about the prospects for the future of their church that they began to wonder if their twenty years of pioneering had been all in vain. The country was losing its independence to Japan. Missionaries were tired. The Korean Christians, like the Ephesians, seemed to have "abandoned the love [they] had at first" (Rev. 2:4 RSV). Then it was that a Canadian medical doctor called them not to give up but to pray. And the little prayer meetings and Bible studies he started were the beginnings of the great Korean Revival of 1904–1908.

The coming of power

What happened? What happened was power. God keeps his promises. He promised power to the powerless disciples on the hill outside Jerusalem. They went back into the city and prayed, and the power came. Suddenly, at Pentecost, "a sound came from heaven like the rush of a mighty wind, . . ." (Acts 2:2 RSV). The Spirit came, and life surged within them, as in coals dropped from a fireplace, apparently dead but breaking open in a shower of sparks. The Spirit brought flame back into the blue, bleak hearts of the disciples. It lifted a dispirited little group of ordinary men and women and sent them out to begin to change the world.

But I must confess that the record of that first Pentecost—all wind and fire and many tongues—is a disconcerting passage for a Presbyterian to read today. It smacks too much of hot gospelers and holy rollers, Quakers and Shakers and enthusiasts. It doesn't describe all that is best and most beautiful in Christian worship, does it? And yet the more I read of the history of the church, the more I am impressed with the fact that some of its most creative and effective periods have been precisely those periods when the gospel was "hot" and not when it was most respectable.

If I were to pick my favorite time in medieval Romanism,

it would be the days of that gentle madman, St. Francis of Assisi. And some of the greatest moments of Protestantism were the times of Puritan enthusiasts and "great awakeners" like Jonathan Edwards. Quakers really quaked once, in the days of their intense beginnings; and when Methodism burned its way into the history of England and America, strong men and women roared and shook under the power of preachers like Wesley and Whitefield and Peter Cartwright. Long-haired dandies would come to Cartwright's camp meetings. "They came to scoff," he wrote, "but they stayed to pray." Suddenly seized by the power, their backs would bend almost to the breaking, then, the tension suddenly released by the peace of the Spirit, they would straighten up with such force that their long hair cracked like whips. Strange, bizarre, a little frightening.

But as someone has said, "The church of Christ has had more power when the world thought it was drunk, as at Pentecost, than when the world thought it was dead." And before we condemn the outer extravagances of those meetings it might be well to ask some questions. Was all that excitement necessary for a renewal, and when renewal does occur, what is the inward, quickening power that produces it?

Not all revivals are fiery, and renewal can be as quiet as an unspoken thought. Almost always revival and renewal begin with prayer, and the best prayers are usually quiet. The revival of 1857 in New York, for example, was just a prayer meeting: no fire, no shouting. As J. Edwin Orr described it, Jeremiah Lanphier, a city missionary in lower Manhattan "passed out handbills inviting anyone interested to join from 12 to 1 on Wednesdays for a prayer meeting. [They could] come for an hour or just five minutes. The first day six people came, the next day forty. Then [they made] it a daily instead of weekly meeting and within six months ten thousand business men were gathering [every day] for prayer in New York City. Within two years one million converts had joined American churches." Just a prayer meeting, but what a prayer meeting!

The Great Revival in Korea was another matter. There was nothing low key about it. It began with quiet prayer meetings, yes, but when it exploded into waves of wailing and weeping and writhing in agonies of confession, the missionaries were terrified. They stopped the meetings.

But the meetings actually could not be stopped. They started again and gradually even the most traditional-minded missionaries recognized that however disturbing its manifestations might appear, the power was not to be feared, and could not be resisted. It came from God.

There is no one way to describe the power. Sometimes it shakes and shouts. Sometimes the quiet words describe it best, words like "cleansing" and "joy" and "love."

For God's power is a cleansing power. Pentecost is rightly described as a filling of the Spirit, but before the filling there was an emptying. Peter knew. On a dark night not long before Pentecost, he felt the pain of the emptying. He heard a cock crow twice, and struck by the enormity of his sin, he "broke down and wept" (Mark 14:72 RSV). No cleansing; no power. So when the crowd, cut to the quick by his preaching, cried, "What shall we do?" Peter said, "Repent." Power without repentance is the wrong kind of power. "Repent," said Peter, "and be baptized . . . in the name of Jesus Christ for the forgiveness of your sins; and you shall receive the gift of the Holy Spirit" (Acts 2:37, 38 RSV).

That is how it happened in Korea too. Here is how a

Korean minister who was there described it: "It was a great sign and wonder. . . . I saw some struggling to get up then falling back in agony. Others again bounded to their feet to rid their souls of some long-covered sin. It seemed unwise that such confessions be made. . . . But there was no help for it. We were under an awful and mysterious power, helpless—missionaries as well as Koreans."

Those were Presbyterians he was describing. That is surprising, perhaps, but no less surprising than a fact which is closely related to it. Now, only eighty years later, there are more Presbyterians in Korea than in the United States. First the repentance, then the cleansing, then the power.

The power of the Spirit is also the power of a great joy. One of the historians of the early days of Christianity has written, "Unless [you] can understand the constant mood of victorious, jubilant happiness . . . [you] simply will not understand primitive [New Testament] Christianity." The crowds watching the disciples at Pentecost thought they were drunk. But they were not intoxicated with wine; they were God-intoxicated. The Spirit had come to dwell with them, and they were overcome; they were "surprised by joy."

The power of the Spirit is also the power of a great love. First God's love: "In this is love," wrote John, "not that we loved God but that he loved us . . ." (1 John 4:10 RSV). It is not a love we manufacture; it is given by the Spirit to all who receive it. "The fruit of the Spirit is love" (Gal. 5:22 RSV). Even the enemies of those early Christians noticed this. "See how they love one another," they said. It was not a separating stroke of lightning, but a warm, uniting love.

But there was more to the love than Christians loving each other. It was a love that broke out beyond the bounds of the church, particularly to the poor, the sick, and the oppressed. The greatest single tribute paid to those early Christians was a remark attributed to one of their most implacable enemies, Julian, the apostate emperor. He is said to have complained, as if the Christians were taking unfair advantage of him, "These Christians feed not only their own poor, but ours as well."

So there was cleansing and joy and love in the power that came at Pentecost. The power was not the wind and not the fire. The power is the Spirit who, with the Father and the Son, is the one God who creates, sustains, and energizes all that ever was or is and will be. He is the promised Power. And he is always there. But an important practical question remains: What is the power for?

Witness and the power

The power is for witness. What happened when the power came that first day of Pentecost in Jerusalem? Peter went out to preach. Pentecost was more than an experience of renewal. It was more than a season of rejoicing. It was a call to mission.

Tradition tells us that every one of the inner circle of the eleven disciples at Pentecost became a missionary. John went to Asia Minor, James to the Arabs, Andrew to the Goths, Peter to Rome, and so on. Even doubting Thomas, somewhat reluctantly as usual, went to far-off India. That's why they were called "apostles," which means missionaries, "ones who were sent out." Had not the Lord said, "You shall receive power . . .; and you shall be my witnesses . . . to the end of earth"? Power is for witness and witness is for the whole world.

What happened when the power came in Korea's Great Revival? The Koreans organized a presbytery. I suppose that sounds like an anticlimax. But it was no accident that along with the power of the revival came the organization of the first presbytery of a Korean Presbyterian Church. The two are not in tension. They belong together. John R. Mott, a great evangelist and a great churchman, organizer, and ecumenical leader, once said "Pray as if there was no such thing as organization, and organize as if there was no such thing as prayer."

The Koreans did both in that great revival year of 1907. They prayed and they organized. They prayed and the power came. They organized—organized the first self-governing, autonomous Korean presbytery—and the presbytery sent out its first missionary, a Korean.

That story deserves a little more detail. It was at that first presbytery meeting that the first seven graduates of the little theological seminary, which had been founded a few years earlier, were to be ordained. They were daunted by the spiritual responsibilities this would bring to each of them. Then another thought occurred to them. Just as they were about to go into the meeting, one of them said, "We will be the first Korean ministers of the Korean church. But a real church has more than ministers. It has missionaries." And they looked hard at a burly young man who had started a little late in their seminary class. "You stoned the first missionary you ever saw, didn't you?" they asked. And he hung his head. It was true. "Then you are going to be our first missionary," they said. And the moderator of the presbytery, my father, who happened to be the missionary that man had stoned sixteen years before, ordained him. The church sent him off as their own first missionary, to a strange island off the southern coast where he in turn was stoned when he stood up to preach the gospel.

Power is for witness, and if we are skeptical about associating Presbyterian ecclesiastical structures with spiritual power and missionary witness, we are either underestimating or underemploying one of the Spirit's gifts to us, the gift of organization.

Where is the power?

But where is the power? I love the church and I believe in it. I love our own Presbyterian segment of the body of Christ most of all. But where is the power in Presbyterianism?

At Pentecost, the power in a little group of about one hundred and twenty men and women swept three thousand people into the fellowship in one day. In the American church, according to one estimate, it takes fifty-four Christians working a whole year to bring just one new member into the church. And among Presbyterians we lose more than we win. Has the power gone? I have found more life in this old church than some give it credit for, but I must admit that statistical record is utterly appalling.

Compare it with Korea. In 1974 there were 1.5 million Presbyterians in Korea. Ten years later, in 1984, there were between 4 and 5 million. Now I do not worship statistics of church growth. I know they are often wrong, and I also know there are tares in all that wheat. But it says something about the distribution of spiritual power in the two churches, here and there, that while Korean Presbyterians were tripling their membership, American United Presbyterians were losing about a third of ours and cutting back on the number of our overseas missionaries at the same time.

Has the power gone? I came across a comment in a letter from Africa which helps me answer that question.

The letter was from some African evangelists telling how they preached the gospel there in East Africa. This is what they said. "We did not begin to preach until we had called for the power of God. That power came. We took it and went forth to preach, and people came confessing Jesus like the fish of the sea in number."

They took it and went forth to feed the hungry. Two-thirds of the world still goes to bed hungry every night. They took it and went forth to heal the sick. Most of the people in this world are suffering and in pain. They took it to open the eyes of the blind—not just the physically blind. One half of the adult population of the world is illiterate and cannot read the Word of God. They took it and went forth to bring justice and freedom to the world's oppressed. More than half of the world's people live under oppression and injustice.

We can and should join in the struggle against all the world's other ills—hunger, sickness, suffering, slavery— but that will still not fulfill the mission. Yet unmet will be the deepest need of all. Two-thirds of the world is still without effectual knowledge of our Lord and Savior Jesus Christ.

The trouble is not the power. The power is still there. The trouble is with us. We do not call for the power. And we complain that we don't have it. We are more naive even than the Arab chieftans Lawrence of Arabia brought with him to the Paris Peace Conference. These men of the desert were amazed at many things, but nothing astonished them half so much as the running water in their hotel rooms. They knew the scarcity of water and its value, yet here it was to be had by the turning of a tap, free and seemingly exhaustless. When they prepared to leave Paris, Lawrence found them trying to detach the faucet so that out in their dry deserts they might always have water. He tried to explain that behind the flowing taps were huge reservoirs, and that without this supply the faucets were useless. But the Arabs insisted. They were sure that the magic instruments would give them water forever.

Are we not even more credulous in our Christian lives? The Arabs expected water from unattached faucets. We look for water to run from a closed tap. In the Holy Spirit are deep reservoirs of power, wells of water springing up into everlasting life. But the Holy Spirit cannot flow through a closed tap, he cannot work through an unyielding life.

So open up the taps. The promise is for any who will believe and receive. And when by faith and by grace we turn the taps and the power flows, watch out! The Spirit works when, where, and how he pleases. When the power comes, it is not you but the Spirit who controls the temperature. You may pray for the fire, and he may choose to send a cool, refreshing rain and a still, small voice. Or you may think you will be more comfortable with the still, small voice and sometimes, as in Korea, there comes the fire and the earthquake.

Jesus is still saying to his disciples: "You shall receive power when the Holy Spirit has come upon you; and you shall be my witnesses. . . ." Witnesses to the ends of this dry and thirsty, this sick and hungry, this oppressed, frightened, lost world. You shall be witnesses that the Savior has come, and that he will come again, and that the Spirit is already here.

9
THE HOLY SPIRIT: THE FINGER OF GOD
Leighton Ford

Leighton Ford, formerly the vice-president of the Billy Graham Evangelistic Association, is an evangelist and church leader. He resides in Charlotte, North Carolina.

IT WAS LATE IN 1944. DR. ROBERT OPPENHEIMER, THE FAMED atomic scientist, was quietly reading a book of the poems of John Donne. The phone rang. It was General Kenneth Bainbridge, deputy director of the Manhattan Project. "Oppie," he said, "We've got what we wanted: a site in New Mexico where we can test our bomb. What do you think we should call the site? Do you have a code name?"

Oppenheimer reflected on the Donne poem he was reading, one referring to the "three-person'd God," and then suggested, "Trinity. We'll call it Trinity."

And now, forty years later, fifteen years before the twenty-first century, many of us wonder if humankind can survive the destructive power on which Oppenheimer and Bainbridge labored. We Christians wonder: What does the power of the holy Trinity mean in confronting the unholy trinity of poverty, hunger, and nuclear weapons build-up, in a world of swelling violence?

It is a desperate hour with desperate needs. Presbyterian Christians now have a reunited church, but we know we must also seek, from God, a reborn church. And only from that rebirth can the renewing power of the Holy Spirit flow, in healing grace, into the broken relationships of our nation and our world. Sam Shoemaker repeatedly said, "When the Person of Jesus touches the problems of the world, then power is born." To see the problems without the Person breeds despair. And if we focus only on the Person, then we can become smug and isolated. But when the Person of Jesus touches the problems, then power is born.

God's power at work

This is true of the incident recorded in Luke 11. Jesus touches the mute man. The demon is cast out. The man speaks, and the crowd questions. Some say, "By Beelzebub, the prince of demons, he is driving out demons" (v. 15 NIV). Others test Jesus by asking for a sign from heaven.

When God works in power, there may be controversy. There was in Jesus' day. There is today. Some would now treat most manifestations of the Spirit's power as dangerous, divisive, and perhaps demonic. When we do so we can become encased in a hard and lifeless orthodoxy. I remember what John Mackay once said of the Pentecostals in Latin America: "Uncouth life is preferable to aesthetic death."

The opposite mistake is to applaud every so-called

manifestation of the Spirit without "testing the spirits." Then we fall into subjectivism and emotionalism. Jesus did not say, "Blessed are those who have an experience." He said, "Blessed rather are those who hear the word of God and obey it" (Luke 11:28 NIV).

It is clear, from the manner in which Jesus answered his critics, that the Holy Spirit was involved in this controversial incident. "Any kingdom divided against itself will be ruined. . . . But if I drive out demons by the finger of God, then the kingdom of God has come to you," he said (Luke 11:17, 20 NIV). In the parallel account in Matthew 12, Jesus refers to this "finger of God" as "the Spirit of God." Of course, God doesn't have literal, physical hands and fingers, but in some sense the Spirit of God is the finger of God at work. The Spirit's activity is God's activity. The Spirit's power is God's kingdom breaking in and setting the captives free. Since controversy often surrounds the work of the Spirit, we may wonder: who, exactly, is the Holy Spirit?

Who is the Holy Spirit?

The Holy Spirit is God's power at work, and the Spirit is not an "it" or an "influence" that can be bought. God does not sell his power to the highest bidder. Neither is the Spirit simply a gift. The question is not, "How much do *I* have of 'this' or 'it'?" The question is, "How much does *he*—God the Spirit—have of me?"

Recently I received a letter of appeal from a television evangelist or, more accurately, a TV peddler. Inside his letter was a pink, plastic surgical glove. The letter called it the "Bible miracle hand of God." There were instructions: "I want you to get this hand out of the pink envelope, put your hand inside. As an act of faith touch the picture of a loved one who is sick or hurting where it hurts. If you need a money miracle, hold your checkbook while you are wearing this miracle hand. If you are hurting, touch the spot where it hurts. Use this powerful hand of God as I have instructed, then mail it back to me along with a faith donation no later than 7:21 P.M. tomorrow night."

I laughed at it and ridiculed it. But then I wondered how many times I have tried to buy or control the Spirit. We sophisticated Presbyterians have our own ways of trying to control the hand of God. We theologize, agonize, and organize. We try to box God into our systems, to predict his every move and know no surprises from him.

Yet God is a free Spirit, as unpredictable as the wind.

The Spirit is sovereign, with his own sense of timing, his own giving and moving. Yet this free, mysterious, sovereign Spirit relates to us in terms we can understand. "God lisps to us," Calvin said, "as a nursemaid to her child." So that we may understand, God's Spirit is comparable to our ordinary fingers, to the ten tools we use to accomplish our most mundane tasks.

This is the paradox of the Spirit. He is totally divine, not just the human spirit heightened in some way. But he works in us, the totally human. As Paul taught, we work, yet not we, but the grace of God works in us (Phil. 2:12, 13). The Holy Spirit is God's Spirit, but he is not alien to our human spirit.

I've had the experience when preaching, counseling, or writing, of having the words come suddenly. Ideas and insights gush out. They seem far beyond anything I've thought of or could have created. They come not from me but through me. And yet at that very moment, I don't feel as if some alien spirit has taken possession of me. I feel more truly myself, more truly and deeply the Leighton

Ford that God made me to be. The paradox of the Spirit is that I work, yet not I, but God works in me.

There is a confusion. We are called to minister in a secularized and paganized world. The secularized world admits no spiritual power. The paganized world admits any spiritual power. It is therefore absolutely essential that the church manifests the authentic spiritual power of the Holy Spirit. We must ask, then, how does the finger of God work? Where do we find it? The answer is not as difficult as we might think. To learn how the finger of God works and where we can find it, we can consider simply what fingers do. What ordinary people do with ordinary fingers suggests several things about the work of the finger of God.

We beckon with our finger and so does God

One thing we do with our finger is beckon others. We motion and say, "Come here." The Spirit is the beckoning finger of God. The people heard Peter at Pentecost and three thousand came to Christ. Cornelius developed a hunger for God and asked for Peter to tell him about salvation. In our Lord's parable, the prodigal son remembers the food and comfort of his home, and goes back. The people at Pentecost, Cornelius, and the prodigal son—all saw the beckoning finger of God motioning, "Come. Come home."

In our world today, God's finger is still beckoning. In Africa, the church is growing at the rate of twenty thousand persons per day. In southeast Asia, refugees torn loose from any security turn to the Lord. In Africa and Asia, they see the beckoning finger of God. And if we expect a new movement of evangelism and church growth in America, it will only happen by the beckoning finger of God. It is God who beckons, not we. As theologian Richard

Lovelace has written, "Our task as evangelists is . . . that of midwives and not that of parents. It is not our responsibility to get people regenerated, but simply to present a consistent witness . . . , to appeal for commitment to Christ, secure . . . that his sheep will hear his voice and follow him because his Spirit will open their hearts to do so."

We write with our fingers and so does God

I am lefthanded. I was making notes at an airport one day, and someone who saw me said, "Do you know that research shows that lefthanded people are more creative and innovative than normal people?"! Whether lefthanded or "normal," people write with their fingers.

So does God. What gave Peter and John the courage that made the rulers realize that these unschooled men had been with Jesus? What created in the first evangelists a fellowship which transcended all barriers and transformed characters? It was the Holy Spirit writing Jesus into their lives. "You are a letter from Christ," said Paul, "the result of our ministry, written not with ink but with the Spirit of the living God, not on tablets of stone but on tablets of human hearts" (2 Cor. 3:3 NIV).

The Puritans often said, "You cannot embrace half a Christ." We cannot trust a Savior who accepts us, without following a Lord who transforms us. Gottfried Osei-Mensah, the African church leader, was converted to Christ because of a headmaster at a school he attended as a young man. He was first impressed as he was walking across the grounds one day and the headmaster greeted him by name. "The Englishmen never bothered to learn our name," said Gottfried. "But this one did."

Gottfried was impressed a second time. The headmaster

had a Bible class every Friday night. Gottfried was a shy boy, but one evening he attended. The room was full and, with no place to sit, he started to walk out. The headmaster saw him and called, "Gottfried, come here. There's a chair for you." The headmaster presented a chair and, said Gottfried, "To my utter mortification, he sat on the floor."

These two simple acts impressed Osei-Mensah and led him to Christ. Years later he saw the headmaster in England and told him what his actions meant to him. But they were so simple and unconscious the headmaster didn't remember them at all. Jesus Christ had been written into the headmaster's life. God uses his finger to write.

We grip with our fingers and so does God

We beckon and write with our fingers, but we also grip and hold with them. George Beverly Shea, the singer who travels with Billy Graham, gets hundreds of requests for songs. Once, he got one he couldn't bring himself to sing. It was called, "His Grip Don't Slip"—terrible grammar, but tremendous theology.

Consider Stephen, facing the stones of the council, but full of the Spirit, looking up to heaven and seeing Jesus. " 'Lord Jesus, receive my spirit,' " he said, and, " 'Lord, do not hold this sin against them' " (Acts 7:59, 60 NIV). What held him but the gripping finger of the Spirit?

When the tests of life are hard, it is a strength to know God's Spirit will hold us fast. "I give them eternal life, and they shall never perish; no one can snatch them out of my hand" said Jesus (John 10:28 NIV). The Spirit assures us (Rom. 8:16) and seals us (Eph. 1:13), and in this security we can venture beyond our own security into evangelism, compassion, and the search for justice.

John Perkins, founder of the pioneer evangelical

community, Voice of Calvary, a holistic ministry in rural Mississippi, left the state three decades ago when his brother was shot by the state police. Settled in California, Perkins went into business. But one day his son went to Sunday school and came home singing about Jesus. His curiosity aroused, John went to the church. In time, he turned to Jesus and then sensed God calling him back to Mississippi. It was the early 1960s. How could a black man risk going back into the midst of the racial turmoil? How could any of us risk such a thing? Only, as John Perkins did, by knowing that the finger of God gripped him and held him. The Spirit gives us that security.

We point with our fingers and so does God

I'm not very mystical. Sometimes I'd like to see more visions, hear more voices. But something did happen in the summer of 1984, at a stadium in Birmingham, England. There I spoke to thousands of people at an overflow meeting of a Billy Graham Crusade. I said a word of greeting and started to go inside when a man named Gerald stopped me. He didn't know anything about me, but he asked if Billy Graham had any literature for bereaved parents.

Gerald had lost a daughter when she was twenty years old. My son, Sandy, died at twenty-one, so we were two men with a common pain. For thirty minutes we talked. Then we prayed. After I had gone back inside, I thought, *Why didn't I ask him if he wanted to give his life to Christ?* When I went back outside, I saw thousands of people milling around, but I found Gerald on the side of a hill. I went and asked him if he wanted to go to Christ, but he said, "I'm not worthy." I had the joy of telling him Christ's acceptance has nothing to do with our worth, and of standing with him as he prayed for Christ to be his Lord.

What pointed him to me, a father who had also lost a child? What pointed me back to him among thousands of people? The Spirit of God points.

Philip was pointed to leave his ministry in Samaria and to go to a desert where an Ethiopian was reading Scripture in his chariot. Peter, a Jewish fisherman, was pointed to a gentile army officer, never knowing the man was hungry for God. Every missionary advance in the book of Acts was initiated by the Spirit.

The Holy Spirit will point to new truths in the Scripture, new understandings of what the church should be, to new areas of ministry, and to people who are looking for him.

We work with our hands and so does God

We type ånd write with our hands. I can't talk without using my hands. We build, sculpt, and mold with our hands. And so does God. The power of the Spirit is power with a purpose.

The psalmist said the heavens were created by the finger of God (Ps. 8:3). That is the creative power of God. Jesus said demons were cast out by the finger of God (Luke 11:20). That is the redemptive power of God.

God continues both his creative and redemptive work through us. He said Bezalel was filled with the Spirit to be an artisan and "make artistic designs" (Exod. 31:3, 4 NIV). Physicist Robert Slocum, on seeing one of the instruments he designed for the Mariner spacecraft, exclaimed, "I've been able to contribute to building God's world." This is God continuing his creative work.

What of God's redemptive work? Pollster George Gallup believes the greatest thing the church could do in America today is to deal redemptively with alcoholism. Psychologists inform us that only a deep conversion can cast out the demons of alcohol and drug addiction. There are also, in our consumer culture, the demons of materialism. The demons of fear keep the leaders of nations from taking risks for peace. I agree with Billy Graham's proposal for Salt X: we should destroy all nuclear weapons. But that cannot happen unless something casts out the demons of fear. The only "something" that can do it is Someone, the Holy Spirit, who will do his redemptive work through us.

The Holy Spirit is God's gift

I asked a friend, a banker, what we need to know about the Holy Spirit. He answered, "I once knew a businessman who was called a counterfeit executive. He dressed like an executive, acted the part, and spoke the part. But he wasn't worth a hoot. He really wasn't an executive." My friend continued, "Too many of us try to play the part of a Christian by ourselves. So I think we need to know there is the power of the Holy Spirit and we need to know he is available."

He is available! We are not on our own. That's what Jesus says in the story of the man who asks his neighbor, "Lend me three loaves of bread." The neighbor is in bed and tries to ignore the beggar. But the asking continues until the sleepy neighbor gets out of bed and gives the shameless beggar some bread. In the same way, said Jesus, "Ask and it will be given to you; seek and you will find; knock and the door will be opened to you" (Luke 11:9 NIV).

There is a hungry world at our doorstep: starving people, needy people, spiritually empty people. We may feel as if there is nothing to give them. But Jesus said his Father isn't a sleepy neighbor. "How much more will your Father in heaven give the Holy Spirit to those who ask him?" (Luke 11:13 NIV).

Sometimes we appear to think that Jesus is a gift freely given to the undeserving, while the Holy Spirit is reserved for status Christians. But the Holy Spirit is not a reward for superlative Christian living. Jesus Christ, by his death and resurrection, did all that was necessary not only for the forgiveness of our sins, but also received the gift of the Holy Spirit and poured him out.

Jesus poured out the Spirit and said, " 'If a man is thirsty, let him come to me and drink. . . . streams of living water will flow from within him' " (John 7:37, 38 NIV). There are two small conditions: that we thirst and come to drink. There is one great condition. The Spirit was not given until Jesus was glorified in his obedience on the cross. Jesus received the Holy Spirit and now gives him to those who thirst.

And we should be thirsty, thirsty for what matters to the Father—the end of our separation from him. We should be thirsty for restoration and celebration. We may be afraid of restoration and renewal: afraid of emotionalism, of losing control, of what the Holy Spirit may call us to do, afraid of seeking justice, even afraid of God himself. Yet God is the Father who gives good gifts to his children, who wants to quench our thirst. He is the loving Father who wants to touch us with the finger of his Spirit.

10
BROTHER JESUS
Thomas W. Gillespie

Dr. Thomas W. Gillespie is the president of Princeton Theological Seminary, Princeton, New Jersey.

WHILE I WAS PASTORING THE PRESBYTERIAN CHURCH IN Burlingame, California, a woman telephoned me at home one night. She was distraught over her life and she needed to talk. Midway through our conversation she said something like this: "You preach Jesus from your pulpit. Week after week you encourage people to believe in him. You urge us to trust him with our lives. I wish I could do that, but I cannot. The Jesus I know is not the friend you make him out to be. My Jesus is an awesome figure. He is so far above and beyond me that he frightens me to death. In his presence I feel more condemned than forgiven, more judged than loved. How can I trust and believe in someone who makes me feel like that?"

As we talked, it became evident that the Jesus she knew was the Jesus portrayed to her by the church of her childhood. He was a Jesus so divine as to be inhumane, so perfect as to be heartless, and so exalted as to be unapproachable. And because he was unapproachable, he was unavailable to her then, in her time of great need.

The Jesus of Hebrews

To that woman and to all who share her sad and distorted vision of Jesus, the New Testament's Letter to the Hebrews speaks with special power. In that letter the humanity of Jesus receives an emphasis that is too often ignored in the piety of the church.

Not that there is nothing awesome about Jesus as he is presented in this letter. If it is a "high christology" that you seek, a christology "from above," there is plenty of it here. In Hebrews 2:3, Jesus is confessed as "the Lord," who himself declared "a great salvation." He is the Jesus attested by the disciples, who became apostles, and by God, who attended his public ministry with "signs and wonders and various miracles and by gifts of the Holy Spirit distributed according to his own will" (Heb. 2:4 RSV). To this Jesus "God [has] subjected the world to come" (Heb. 2:5 RSV). Everything has been put in subjection to him, nothing left outside his control. Jesus is here presented as the one "for whom and by whom all things exist, . . ." (Heb. 2:10 RSV). He is "the pioneer" of our salvation, the one who delivers "all those who through fear of death were subject to lifelong bondage" (Heb. 2:15 RSV). He is the "merciful and faithful high priest in the service of God, . . ." who represents God to the world and intercedes for the world to God (Heb. 2:17 rsv). Here then are most of the themes of classical christology—incarnation, ministry, atonement, resurrection, and exaltation. A "high christology" indeed.

Yet the author of the Letter to the Hebrews emphasizes that the identity of Jesus was manifested, and the work of Jesus accomplished, through his humanity. So here also is some christology "from below." Jesus is the One who is unashamed to call us his brothers and sisters, and to make himself our Brother. Since we "share in flesh and blood, he himself likewise partook of the same nature . . ." (Heb. 2:14 rsv). He is the Jesus who is able to sympathize with our weaknesses because he shared them. He is the Jesus who suffered as we suffer. He is the Jesus who died even as we shall die, with the difference that through his death the power of death has been broken.

The humanity of Jesus: how important?

But given the "high christology" of the Letter to the Hebrews, the question is how important this emphasis upon his humanity really is. Dr. Roy Fairchild tells of a senator who gave a speech. Afterwards he was approached by a gushing woman constituent. "Oh Senator," she said, "that speech was wonderful. It was simply superfluous."

"I'm glad you liked it," he responded with tongue in cheek. "I plan to have it published posthumously."

To which she replied, "I hope that will be real soon."

The question is whether the humanity of Jesus, emphasized under the rubrics of temptation, suffering, and death is essential or superfluous to christological conviction.

Douglas John Hall believes that it is clearly essential. In his insightful book, *Lighten Our Darkness,* he notes that the same emphasis is made by the Apostle Paul under

the theme of "Christ crucified." In fact, Hall argues, the
test of theological authenticity is whether we can present
Jesus as *the crucified*. He formulates the issue in a series
of pressing questions:

Can one perceive in the Jesus of this theology a man
who knows the meaninglessness, . . . the anguish of
hopelessness? . . . Would a man dare to confess to this
Jesus his deepest anxiety, his most ultimate questions?
Would such a Jesus comprehend the gnawing care of
a generation of parents who live every day with the question: Will my children be able to survive as human beings
in the year 2001, 2026? . . . Would he, the God-Man
of this theology, be able to weep over the dead bodies
of little children in Southeast Asia and Brazil, as he wept
over his friend Lazarus? Could he share our doubt; doubt
about God, about man, about life, about every absolute?
. . . Would such a Christ understand failure? Could he
participate in *our* failure? Or is he eternally above all
that? Do we have to do with him now only as the risen
and glorious One, who has put all that behind him?
Magnificent with answers, and himself the Answer, has
he ascended far above the misty flats of our questions?
In sum, the test of authenticity in theology today is: Is
this "Jesus Christ and him crucified?"

To such questions, the author of Hebrews responds with
a resounding *yes!* It is the humanity of Jesus that has been
exalted. His own experiences of temptation and suffering
and death are not left behind or forgotten. They are taken
up with him into his priestly ministry in the service of
God. As Douglas Hall explains it,

The theology of the Cross is first of all a way of speaking
about the character of God's entry into the sphere of
human history. It is not merely a statement about the

death of Jesus, but about his life and the meaning of his life for our lives. . . . It is testimony to the *assumption* of the human condition by the One who created and creates out of nothing. The basic point of this theology is not to reveal that our condition is one of darkness and death; it is to reveal to us the One who meets us in our darkness and death. It is a theology *of the Cross*, not because it wants to put forward this ghastly spectacle as a final statement about life in this world, but because it insists that God, who wills to meet us, love us, redeem us, meets, loves, and redeems us precisely where we are; in the valley of the shadow of death. The theology of the Cross declares *God* is with you—Emmanuel. *He* is alongside you in your suffering. *He* is in the darkest place of your dark night.

Both the Apostle Paul and the Letter to the Hebrews would agree that the Jesus proclaimed in the gospel is the One who made our humanity his own. To be sure, he is also the risen and living One. Paul emphasizes the resurrection of Jesus, the author of Hebrews the exaltation, but the point is that as the risen and living One, Jesus remains the One who was tempted, suffered, and died on the cross. And that means that by the presence and power of his Spirit he continues to stand with us in the midst of all the negations and contradictions of life up to and including our death. No matter who you are or what your situation in life, neither you nor your situation are strangers to Jesus. He has been where you are and is available to you where you are. That is what makes him our Brother not merely long, long ago, but here and now. It makes him approachable as our faithful and merciful High Priest in the service of God.

That is why the author of the Letter to the Hebrews

exhorts his readers to avail themselves of this priestly ministry of Jesus: "Let us, then, hold firmly to the faith we profess. For we have a great High Priest who has gone into the very presence of God—Jesus, the Son of God. Our High Priest is not one who cannot feel sympathy for our weaknesses. On the contrary, we have a High Priest who was tempted in every way that we are; but did not sin" (Heb. 4:14, 15 TEV).

Brother Jesus

I almost wish that last line had not been written. I know it is theologically true and necessary, yet I find it personally troublesome. For how do I relate to a Brother who has never done anything wrong? I am an only child, so what little I know about sibling rivalry and relationships is what I have read in books and observed in our own children. But that is enough to convince me that it would be tough to have a brother who was perfect. Others would always be comparing you to him, and you would be comparing yourself to him. It would be demoralizing at best. And it certainly would not do much for your brotherly relationship.

How then does our Brother Jesus avoid having that kind of impact upon our lives? The answer, of course, depends upon how he relates to us. Many years ago I was listening to a radio sermon by a Baptist pastor from St. Louis. He said that he had two brothers. One he described as the brother most like himself. They shared the same interests, the same politics, even the same theology. Consequently, they were close throughout their lives. The other brother he described as the brother least like himself. They had different interests, different views on politics and religion. As a result, they were never close—until one day during the Great Depression. The pastor and his young wife were serving a very small congregation in upstate New York, and his salary was meager. In fact, he was unable to buy coal to heat the manse during the winter. But the day his money ran out, he received a letter in the mail from the brother least like himself. It was a word of love and encouragement, along with a check for one hundred dollars. Now, this radio preacher declared, there is nothing quite like one hundred dollars worth of brotherhood when you are broke and cold.

His point was simple. Even a brother who is in some way quite unlike oneself can be the mediator of God's grace to us. And that is the role Jesus plays in our life. He stands with us as our Brother—not to condemn us by his sinlessness, but to mediate the grace of God to us. In his own obedience to the Father, he does not lord it over us but ministers to us. What he seeks is not his own advantage but ours. That is why we can respond to this wondrous invitation: "Let us be brave, then, and approach God's throne where there is grace. There we will receive mercy and find grace to help us just when we need it" (Heb. 4:16 TEV).

The throne of grace

The throne of grace is open to us through what Karl Barth called "the humanity of God" in Jesus. That is a phrase worth pondering, for it reflects the mystery defined by the Council of Chalcedon when it confessed Jesus to be "truly God and truly human." Because Jesus represents the humanity of God, he is reliable for mercy and grace. Because he represents the *humanity* of God, he is approachable for mercy and grace. Those brave enough to respond to the invitation to "approach God's throne," however, are those who "see Jesus . . . crowned with glory and honor" (Heb. 2:7 TEV). Those who receive mercy and grace through the humanity of Jesus are those who confess that "God [has] subjected the world to come" to Jesus (Heb. 2:5 RSV). Put simply, our confession of who Jesus is and what he has done for the world defines who we are in his church and what we are to do in the world. In terms of our life together, the "humanity of God" means we must be the mediators of God's mercy and grace to one another. And by "one another" I refer to the brothers and sisters who are most like ourselves *and* the brothers and sisters who are least like ourselves. No, *especially* those who are least like ourselves.

It is not difficult to mediate mercy and grace to those brothers and sisters who share our views on theology. We Presbyterians continue to demonstrate just how easy that is as we gather ourselves into like-minded groups. But the test of the authenticity of our witness to Jesus our Brother is the extent to which we are willing and able to mediate God's mercy and grace to the brothers and sisters who are least like ourselves. No matter who wins the struggle for power in the church, it will be in vain if it is won at the price of denying "the humanity of God" given to us in Jesus. The world will not listen, and should not listen, to a church which cannot or will not live its own confession within its common life. In terms of our ministry and mission to the world, "the humanity of God" requires us to enter into the temptations, the suffering, even the death of that world. If that is what makes Jesus approachable, it is also what makes his church credible. The so-called liberation theologians are right on at least one point: orthopraxis is what makes orthodoxy intelligible and believable. And what we are called by the gospel to practice is not merely justice, for justice is the minimum requirement of the Law of God. What we are called to practice under the gospel is the mercy and grace of God, the very mercy and grace that we have ourselves received through the humanity of God in Jesus.

What that requires of us concretely, neither the brothers and sisters most like ourselves nor the brothers and sisters least like ourselves fully know. Let us be honest. The truth is that not one of us alone or even all of us together understands the gospel completely. Perhaps if we begin with that admission, and if we are willing to enter together into the temptations, suffering, and death of the world, perhaps we will discover the answers. Only so will the church ever be renewed.

And to such renewal Jesus, our Brother, calls us.